FOR ORGANS, PIANOS & ELECTRONIC KEYBOARDS

E-Z PLAY® TODAY

355

Smoky Mountain Gospel Favorites

A COLLECTION OF 36 TREASURED HYMNS

CONTENTS

2	Amazing Grace	The Old Rugged Cross	44
4	Are You Washed in the Blood	Pass Me Not, O Gentle Savior	46
6	At Calvary	Power in the Blood	48
8	At the Cross	Rock of Ages	50
10	Beulah Land	Send the Light	37
12	Blessed Assurance	Shall We Gather at the River?	52
14	Church in the Wildwood	Since Jesus Came into My Heart	54
20	Have Thine Own Way Lord	Softly and Tenderly	56
22	I Am Bound for the Promised Land	Standing on the Promises	58
24	I Love to Tell the Story	Sweet Hour of Prayer	60
26	I've Got Peace Like a River	Tell It to Jesus	62
28	In the Garden	There Is a Fountain	64
17	In the Sweet By and By	We'll Understand It Better By and By	66
30	Just as I Am	We're Marching to Zion	68
32	Just Over in the Gloryland	What a Friend We Have in Jesus	74
34	The Lily of the Valley	When the Roll Is Called Up Yonder	71
40	Near the Cross	When We All Get to Heaven	76
42	Nothing but the Blood	Whiter Than Snow	78
		Registration Guide	80

ISBN 978-0-634-00305-9

HAL•LEONARD®
CORPORATION

7777 W. BLUEMOUND RD. P.O. BOX 13819 MILWAUKEE, WI 53213

T0045060

E-Z Play® Today Music Notation © 1975 by HAL LEONARD CORPORATION

E-Z PLAY and EASY ELECTRONIC KEYBOARD MUSIC are registered trademarks of HAL LEONARD CORPORATION.

Visit Hal Leonard Online at
www.halleonard.com

Amazing Grace

Registration 2
Rhythm: Waltz

Words by John Newton
Traditional American Melody

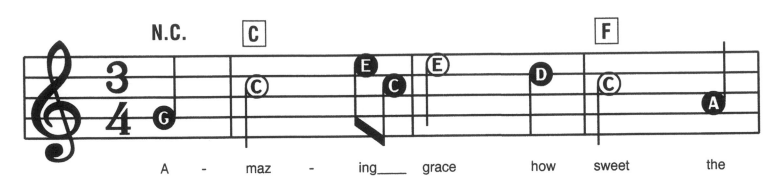

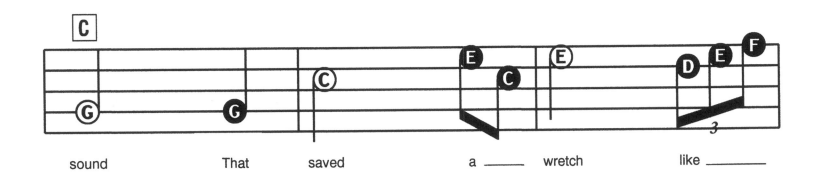

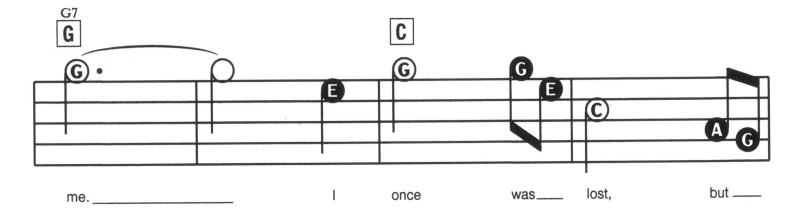

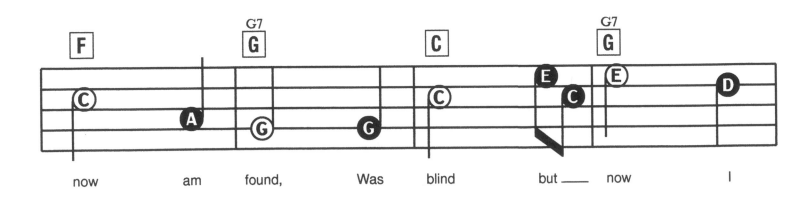

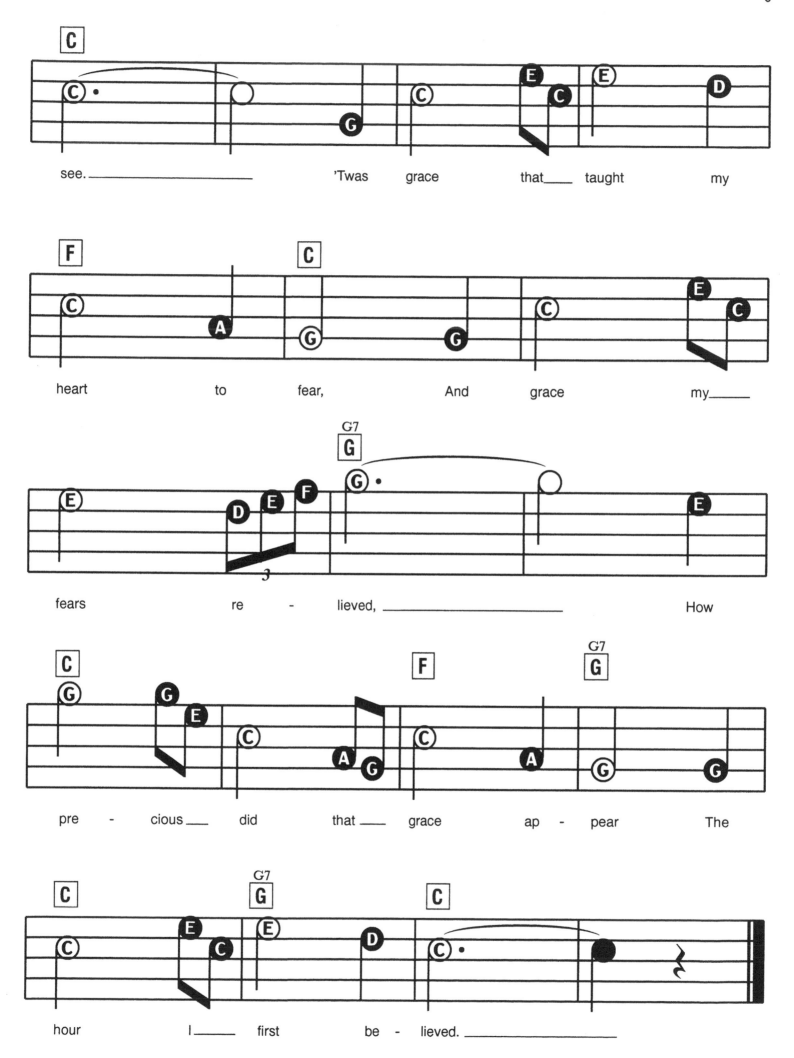

Are You Washed in the Blood

Registration 2
Rhythm: Ballad or Fox Trot

Traditional

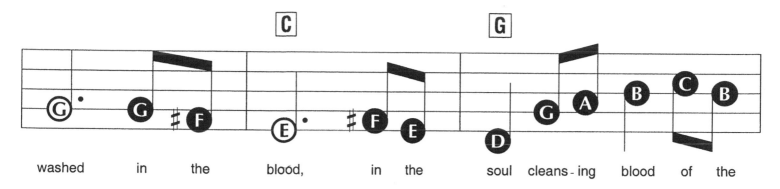

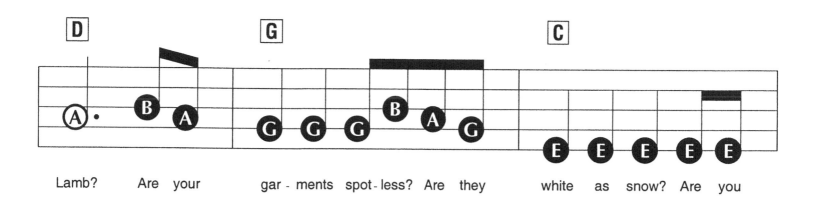

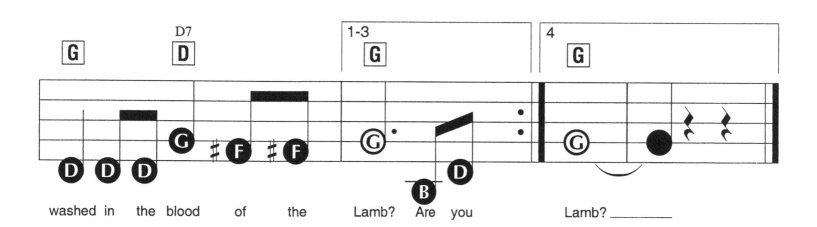

Additional Lyrics

3. When the Bridegroom cometh will your robes be white?
   Are you washed in the blood of the Lamb,
   Will your soul be ready for the mansions bright,
   And be washed in the blood of the Lamb?
   Refrain

4. Lay aside the garments that are stained with sin,
   And be washed in the blood of the Lamb;
   There's a fountain flowing for the soul unclean,
   O be washed in the blood of the Lamb!
   Refrain

At Calvary

Registration 1
Rhythm: Ballad or Fox Trot

Words by William Newell
Music by D.B. Towner

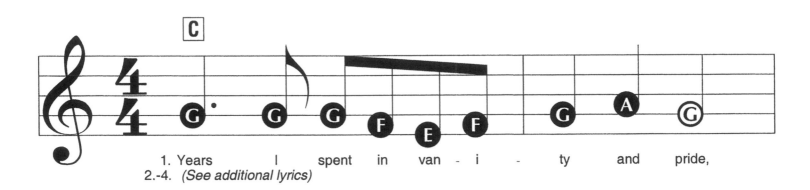

1. Years I spent in van - i - ty and pride,
2.-4. *(See additional lyrics)*

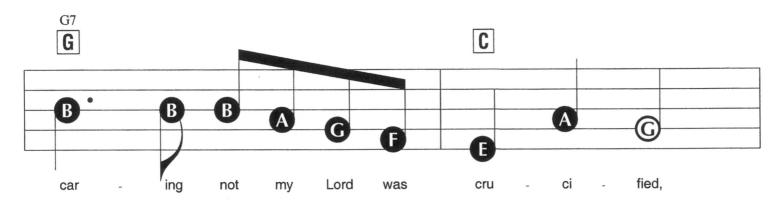

car - ing not my Lord was cru - ci - fied,

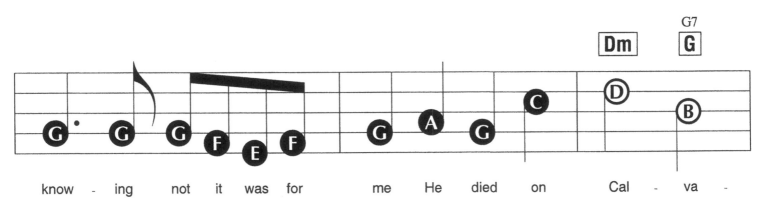

know - ing not it was for me He died on Cal - va -

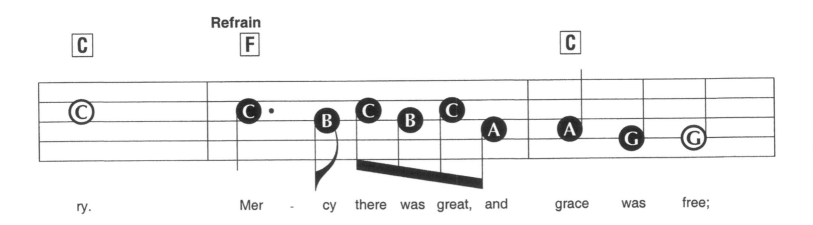

Refrain

ry. Mer - cy there was great, and grace was free;

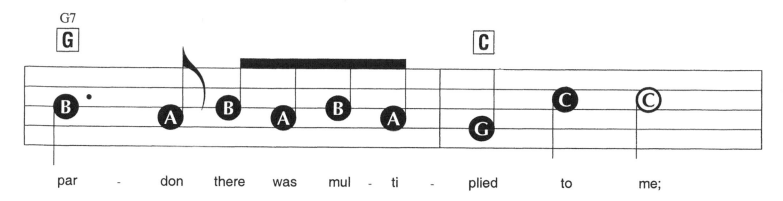

par - don there was mul - ti - plied to me;

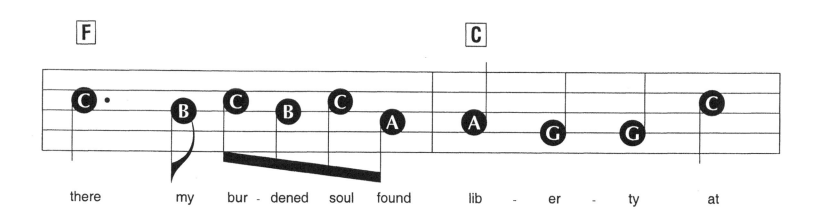

there my bur - dened soul found lib - er - ty at

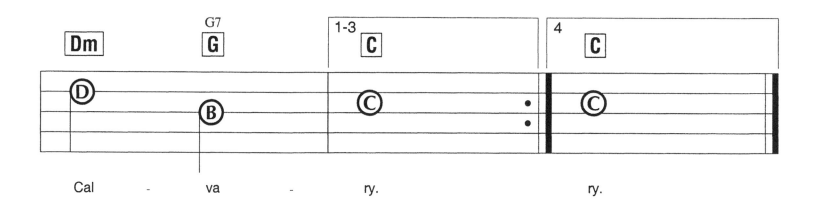

Cal - va - ry.   ry.

Additional Lyrics

2. By God's Word at last my sin I learned;
Then I trembled at the law I spurned,
Till my guilty soul imploring turned to Calvary.
Refrain

3. Now I've giv'n to Jesus ev'rything,
Now I gladly own Him as my King,
Now my raptured soul can only sing of Calvary.
Refrain

4. Oh, the love that drew salvation's plan!
Oh, the grace that bro't it down to man!
Oh, the mighty gulf that God did span at Calvary.
Refrain

At the Cross

Registration 2
Rhythm: Ballad or Fox Trot

Text by Isaac Watts
Music by Ralph E. Hudson

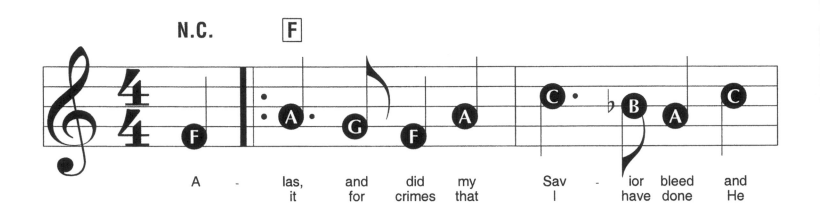

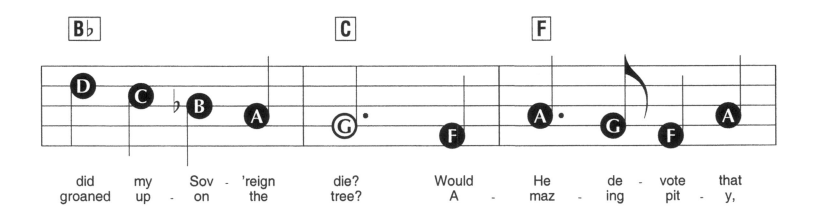

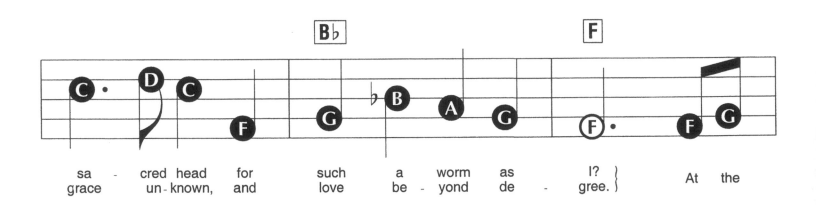

9

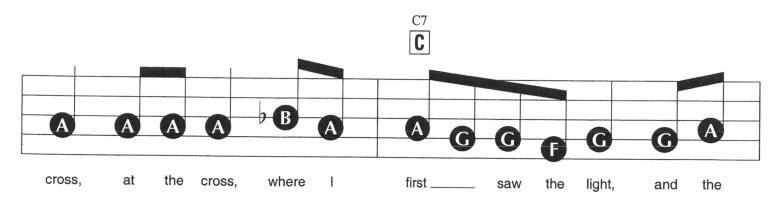

cross, at the cross, where I first _____ saw the light, and the

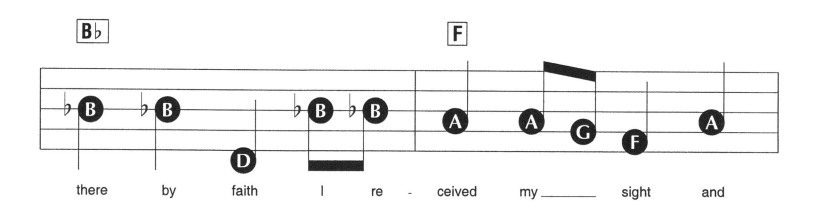

bur - den of my heart rolled a - way, it was

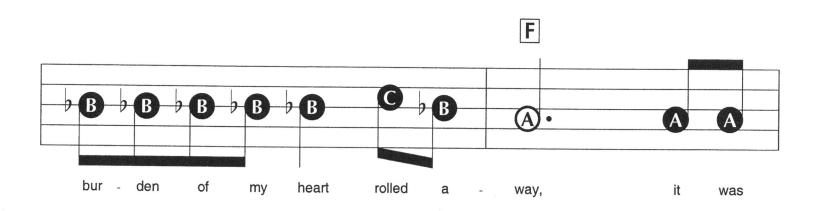

there by faith I re - ceived my _____ sight and

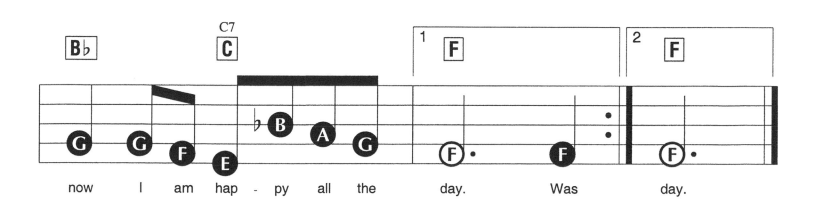

now I am hap - py all the day. Was day.

Beulah Land

Registration 3
Rhythm: Waltz

Words by Edgar Page
Music by John R. Sweney

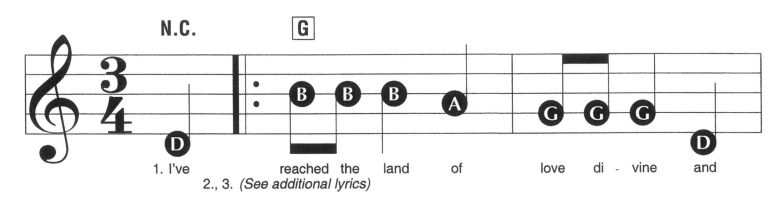

N.C.

1. I've reached the land of love di - vine and
2., 3. *(See additional lyrics)*

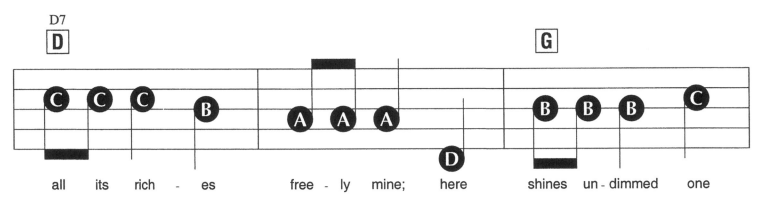

all its rich - es free - ly mine; here shines un - dimmed one

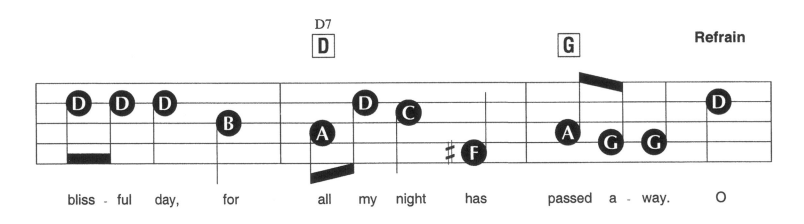

bliss - ful day, for all my night has passed a - way. O

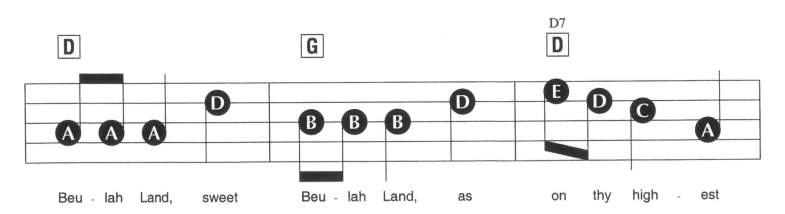

Beu - lah Land, sweet Beu - lah Land, as on thy high - est

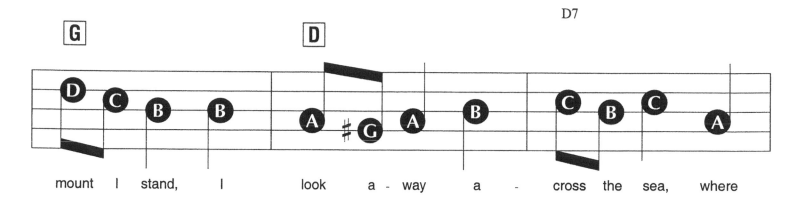

mount I stand, I look a-way a - cross the sea, where

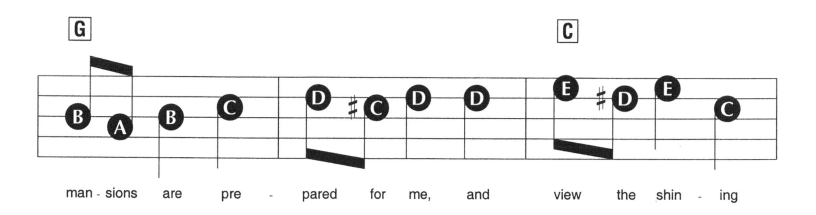

man-sions are pre - pared for me, and view the shin - ing

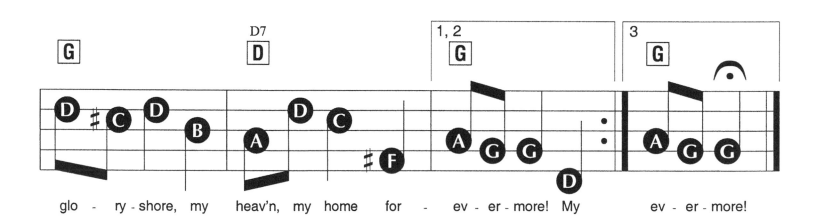

glo - ry-shore, my heav'n, my home for - ev-er-more! My   ev - er - more!

Additional Lyrics

2. My Savior comes and walks with me,
And sweet communion here have we;
He gently leads me by His hand,
For this is heaven's borderland.
Refrain

3. The zephyrs seem to float to me,
Sweet sounds of heaven's melody,
As angels with the white-robed throng
Join in the sweet Redemption song.
Refrain

Blessed Assurance

Registration 6
Rhythm: Waltz

Lyrics by Fanny Crosby and Van Alstyne
Music by Phoebe P. Knapp

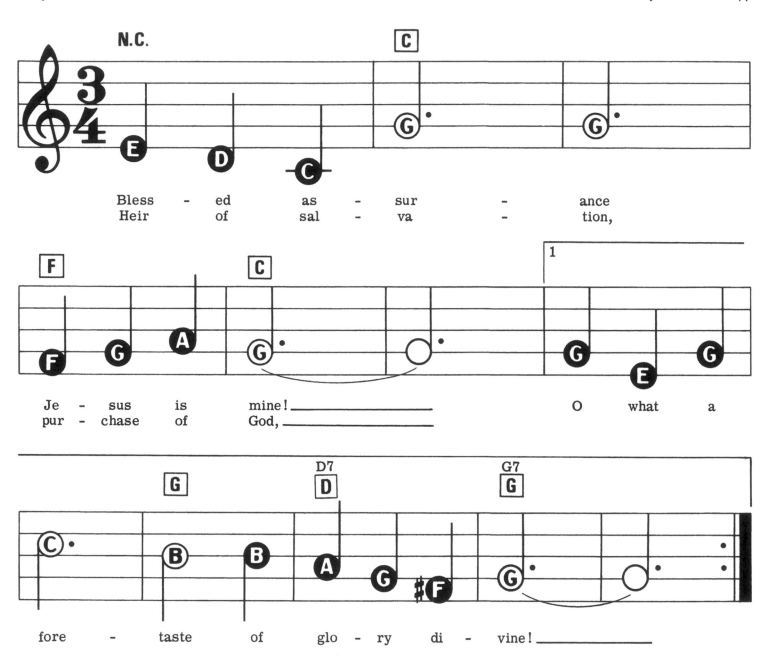

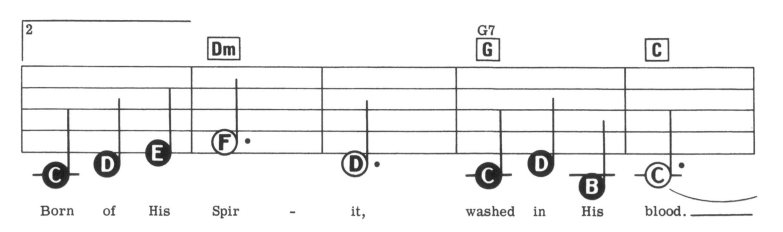

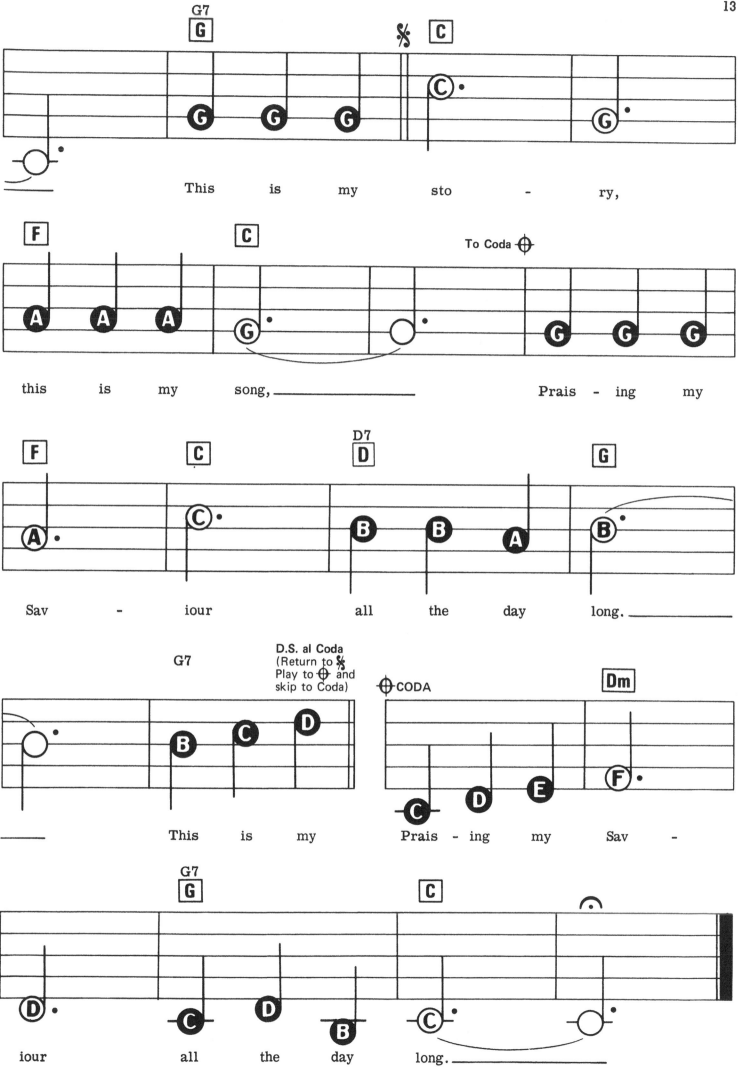

Church in the Wildwood

Registration 2
Rhythm: 8 Beat or Swing

Words and Music by
William S. Pitts

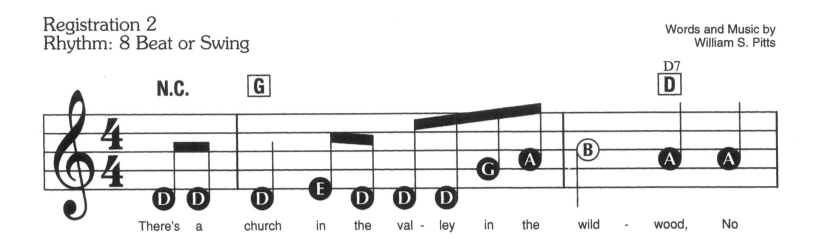

There's a church in the val - ley in the wild - wood, No

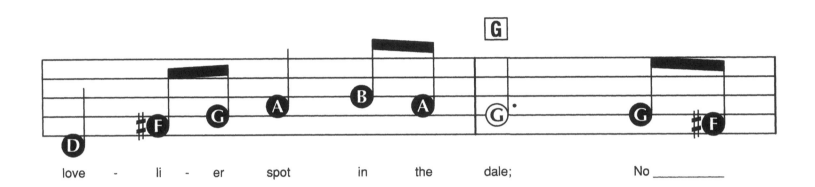

love - li - er spot in the dale; No _____

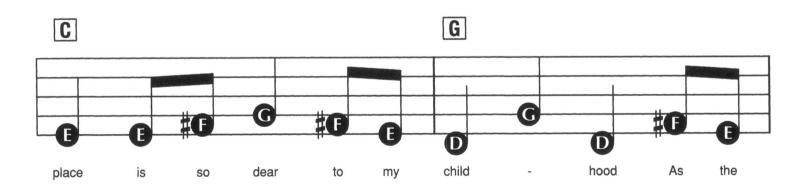

place is so dear to my child - hood As the

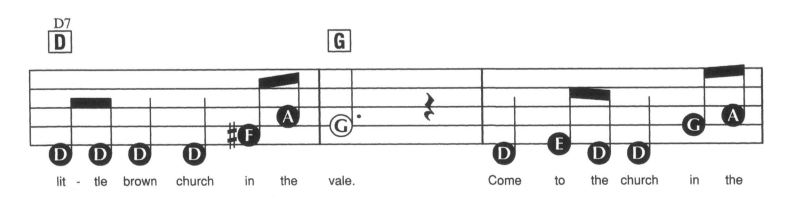

lit - tle brown church in the vale. Come to the church in the

15

16

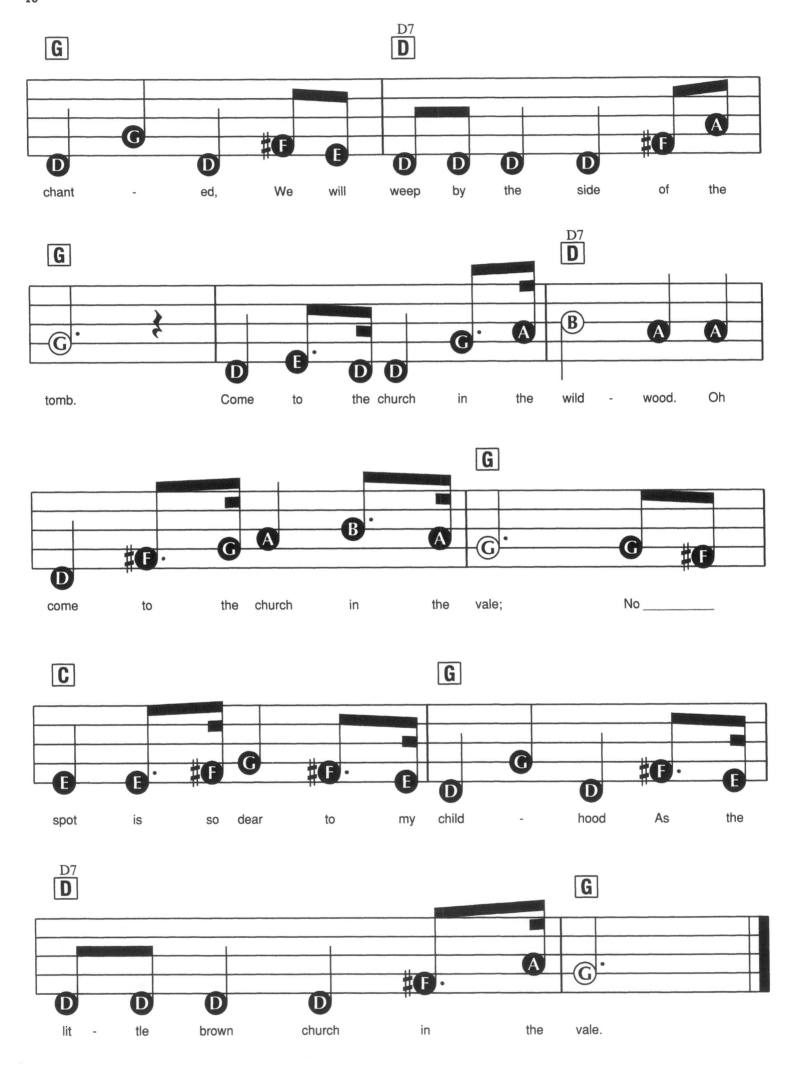

In the Sweet By and By

Registration 1
Rhythm: Rock or Pops

Words by Sanford F. Bennet
Music by Joseph P. Webster

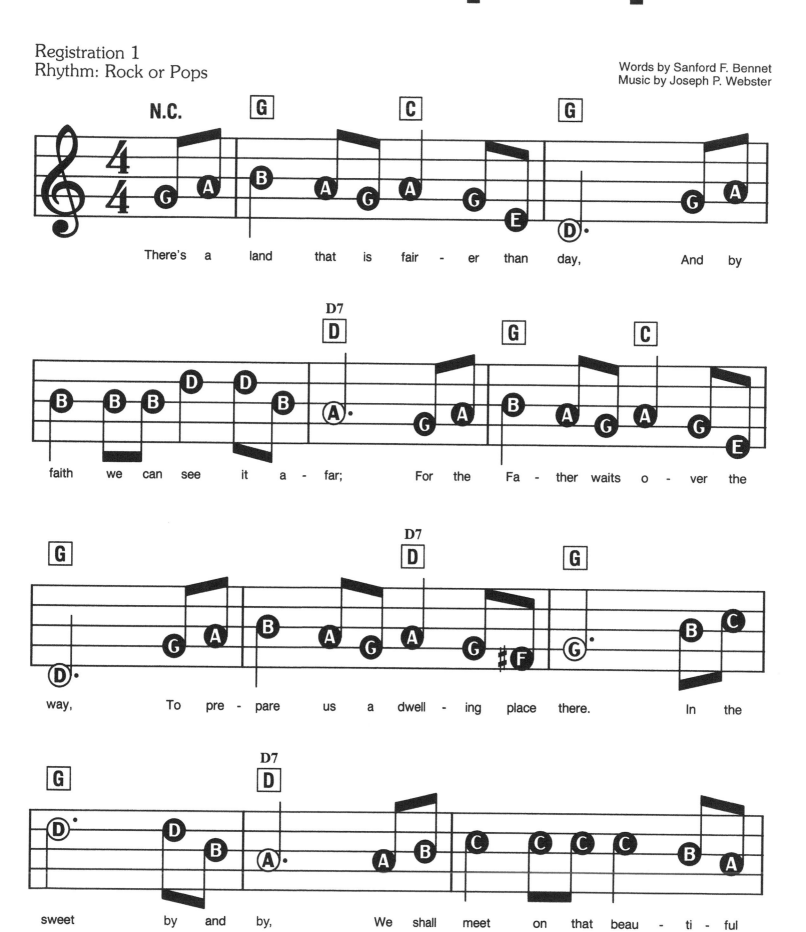

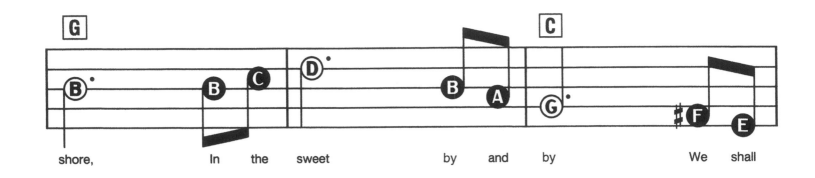

shore,   In   the   sweet   by   and   by   We   shall

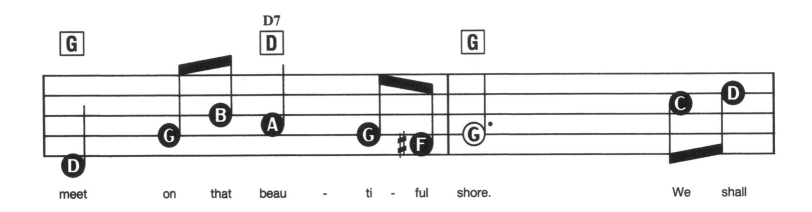

meet   on   that   beau - ti - ful   shore.   We   shall

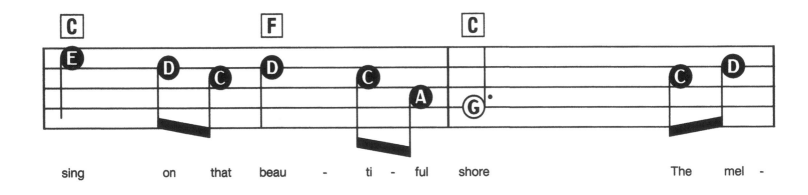

sing   on   that   beau - ti - ful   shore   The   mel-

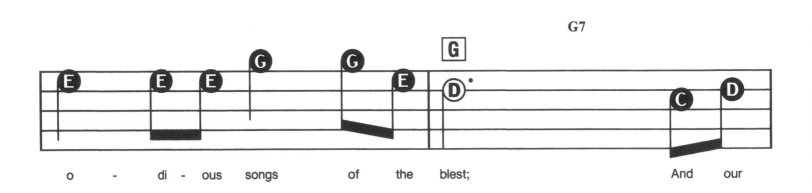

o - di - ous   songs   of   the   blest;   And   our

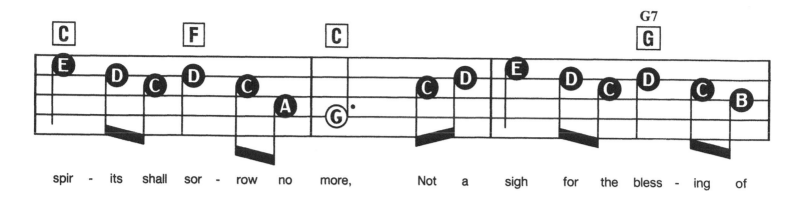

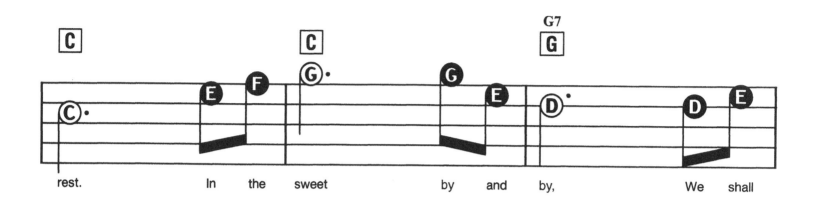

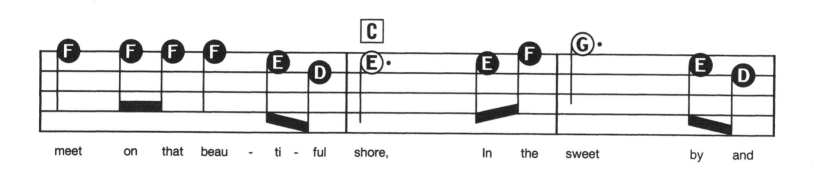

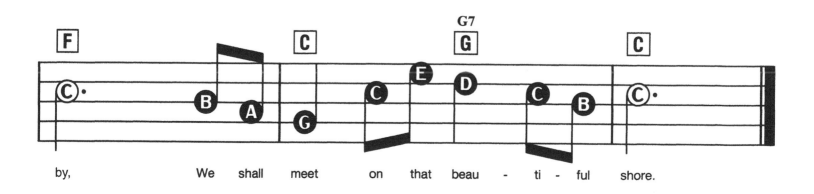

Have Thine Own Way Lord

Registration 3
Rhythm: Waltz

Words by Adelaide Pollard
Music by George Stebbins

N.C.

3/4   A   G   A

B♭   B

F   A   F   E   F

1. Have Thine own   way,   Lord!   Have Thine own
2. way,   Lord!   Have Thine own
3., 4. *(See additional lyrics)*

C7
C

G   O   G   ♯F   G   A

way! _____   Thou   art   the   pot -
way! _____   Search   me   and   try

F

G   G   F   E   F   O

ter,   I   am   the   clay! _____
me,   mas - ter   to -   day! _____

B♭   **F**   **F7**

A   G   A   B   A   C   B   C

Mold   me   and   make   me   af - ter   Thy
Whit - er   than   snow,   Lord,   wash   me   just

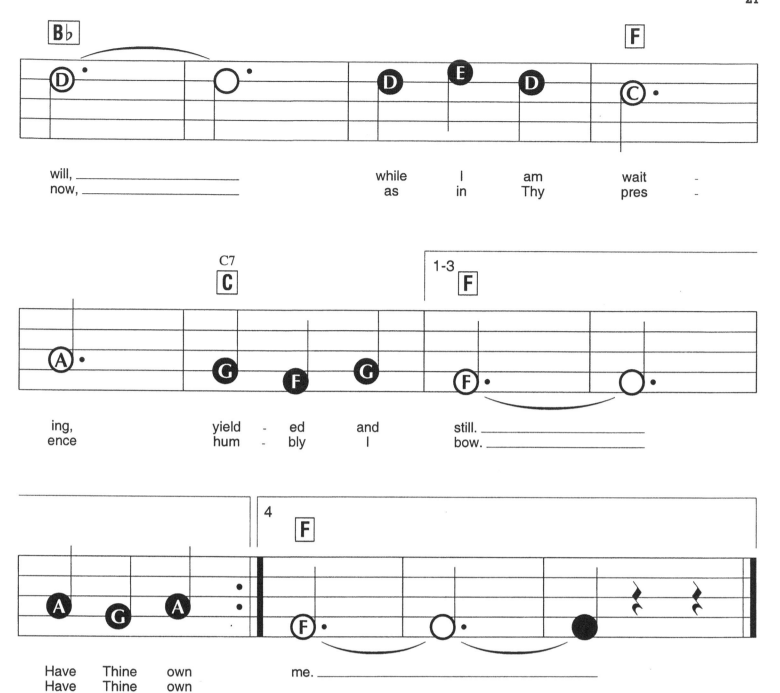

Bb

will,_____
now,_____

while   I   am   wait -
as   in   Thy   pres -

F

C7
C

1-3
F

ing,
ence

yield - ed   and
hum - bly   I

still._____
bow._____

4
F

Have   Thine   own
Have   Thine   own

me._____

Additional Lyrics

3. Have Thine own way, Lord!
   Have Thine own way!
   Wounded and weary, help me, I pray!
   Power, all power
   Surely is Thine!
   Touch me and heal me, Savior divine.

4. Have Thine own way, Lord!
   Have Thine own way!
   Hold o'er my being absolute sway!
   Fill with Thy Spirit
   Till all shall see
   Christ only, always, living in me.

I Am Bound for the Promised Land

Registration 4
Rhythm: Swing

Traditional

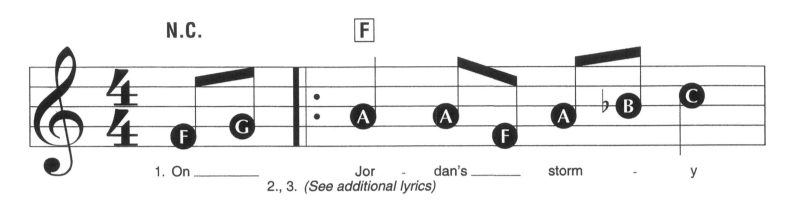

1. On _____ Jor - dan's _____ storm - y
2., 3. *(See additional lyrics)*

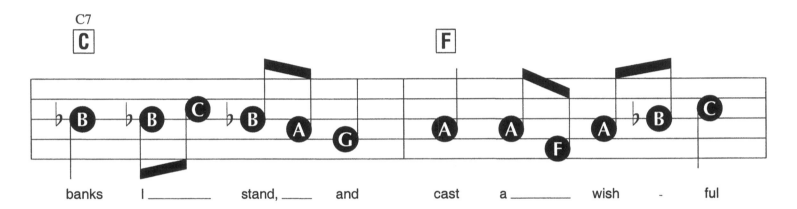

banks I _____ stand, _____ and cast a _____ wish - ful

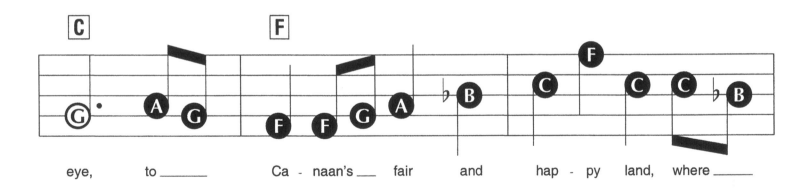

eye, to _____ Ca - naan's _____ fair and hap - py land, where _____

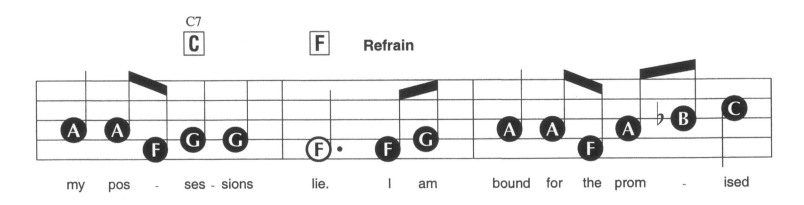

my pos - ses - sions lie. I am bound for the prom - ised

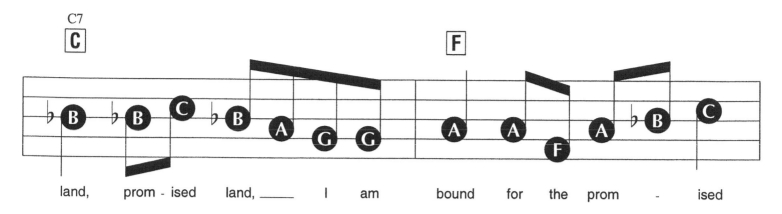

land, prom - ised land, _____ I am bound for the prom - ised

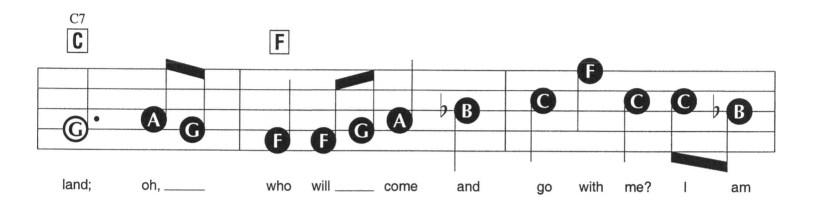

land; oh, _____ who will _____ come and go with me? I am

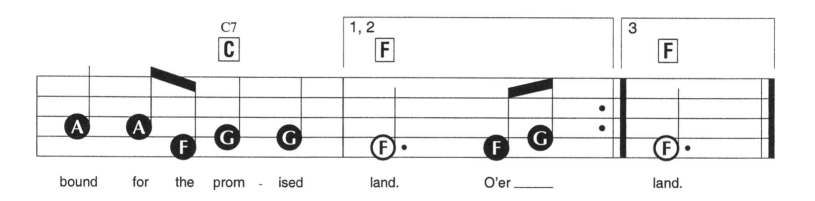

bound for the prom - ised land. O'er _____ land.

Additional Lyrics

2. O'er all those wide extended plains
   Shines one eternal day,
   There God the Son forever reigns
   And scatters night away.
   Refrain

3. When shall I reach that happy place,
   And be forever blest?
   When shall I see the Father's face,
   And in His bosom rest?
   Refrain

I Love to Tell the Story

Registration 4
Rhythm: March

Words by A. Catherine Hankey
Music by William G. Fischer

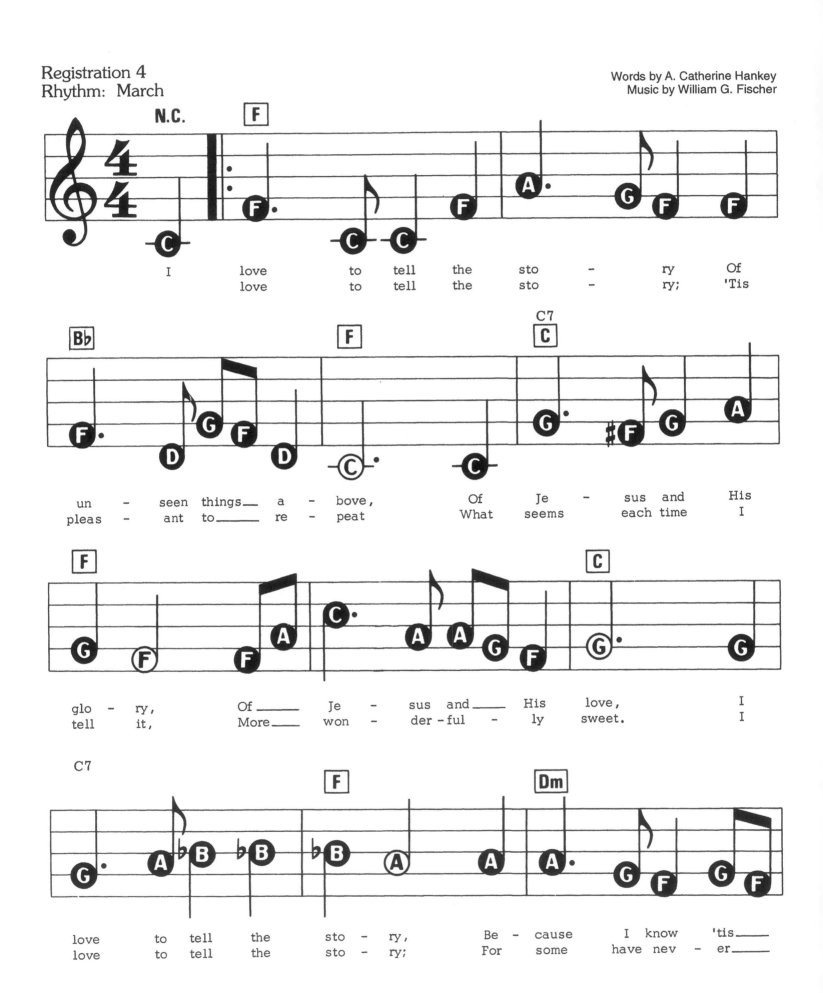

25

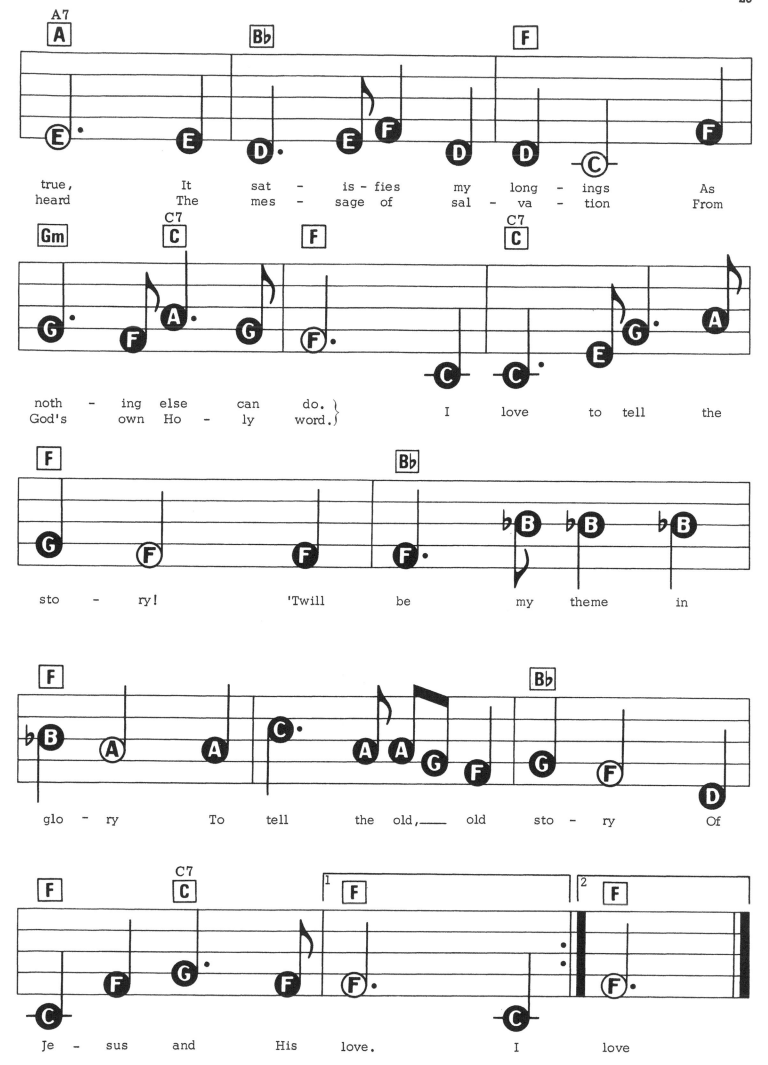

I've Got Peace Like a River

Registration 8
Rhythm: Ballad or Fox Trot

Traditional

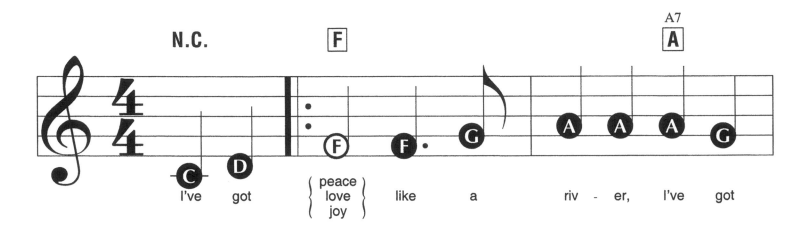

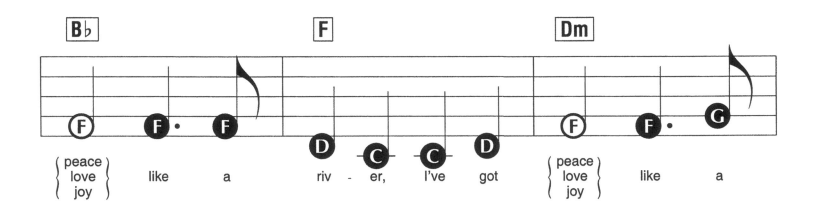

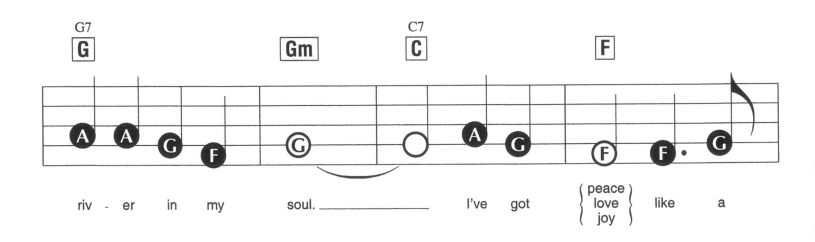

27

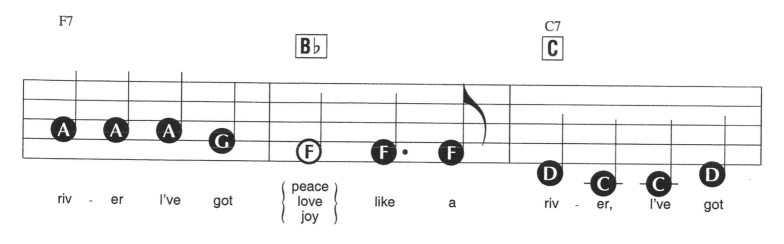

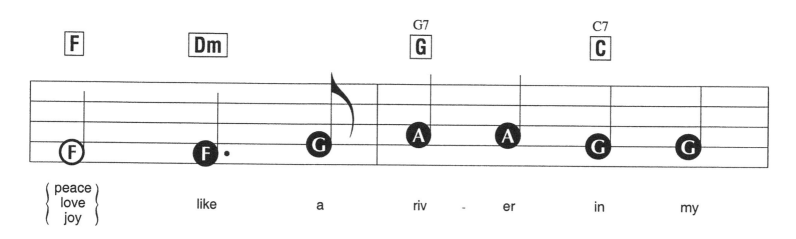

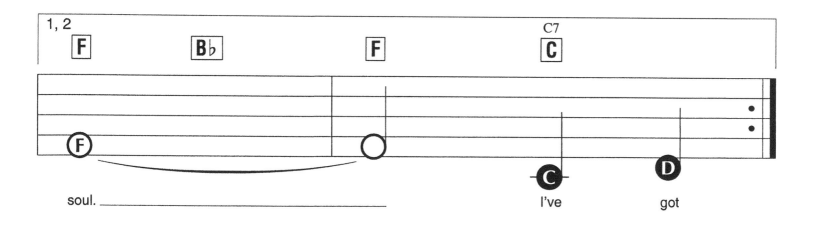

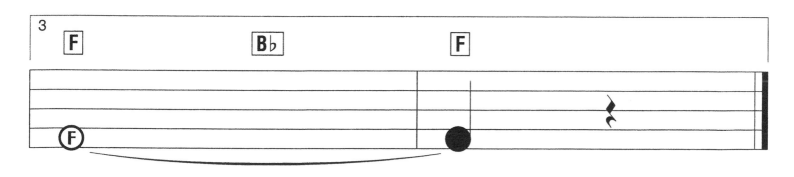

In the Garden

Words and Music by
C. Austin Miles

Registration 2
Rhythm: Waltz

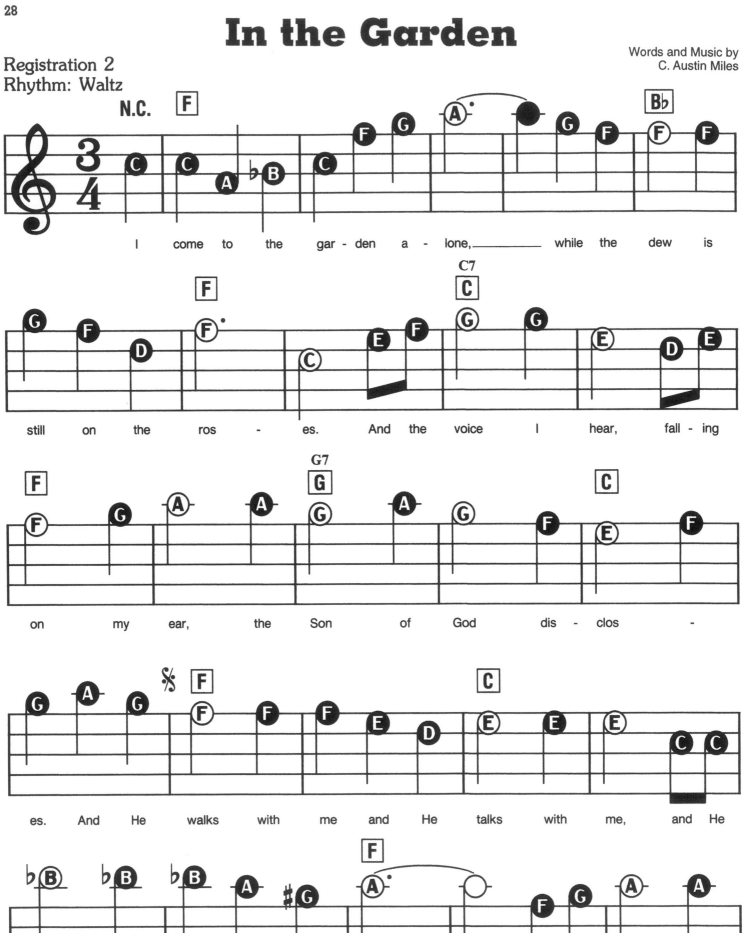

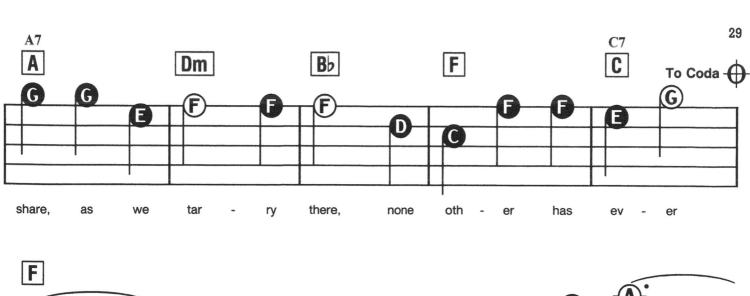

share, as we tar - ry there, none oth - er has ev - er

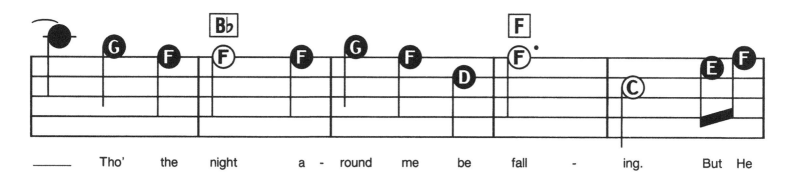

known._____ I'd stay in the gar - den with Him,_____

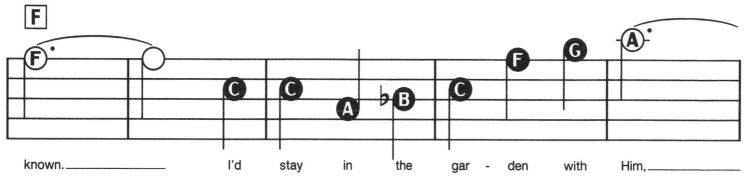

_____ Tho' the night a - round me be fall - ing. But He

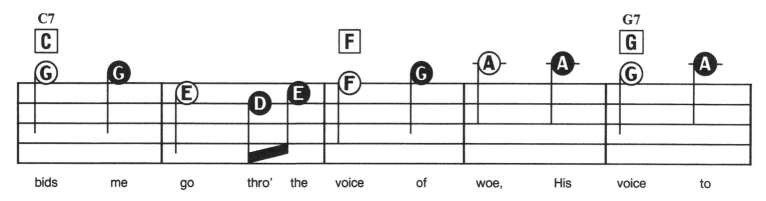

bids me go thro' the voice of woe, His voice to

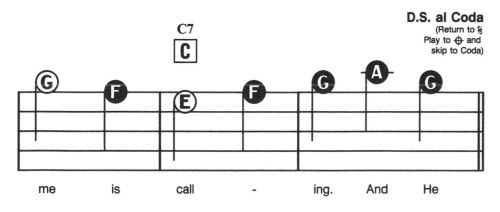

me is call - ing. And He

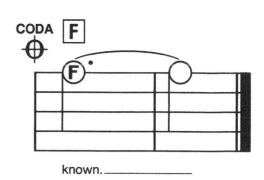

known._____

Just As I Am

Registration 9
Rhythm: Waltz

Words by Carlotte Elliott
Music by William Bradbury

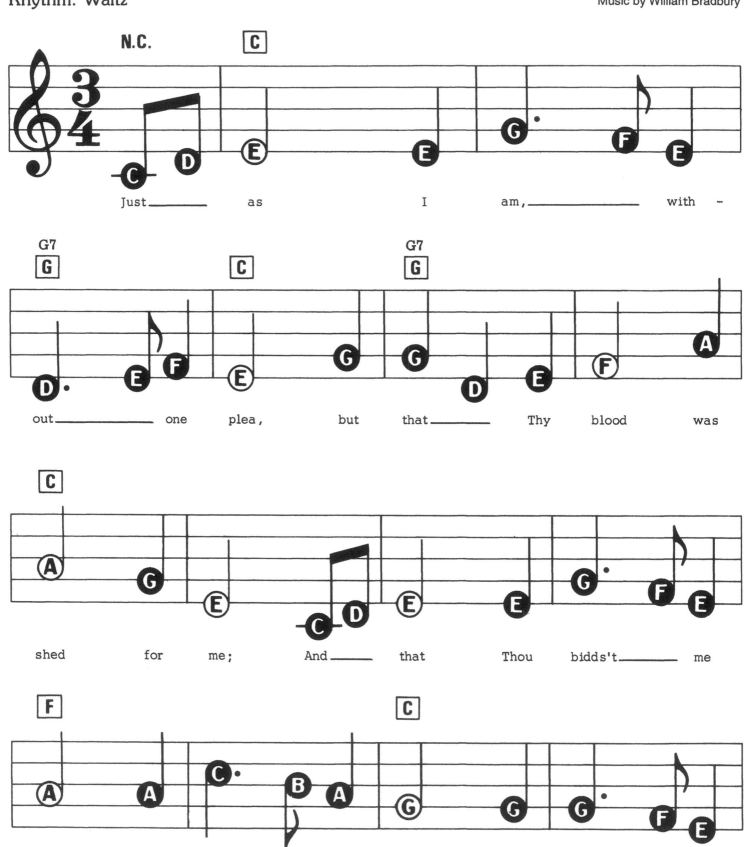

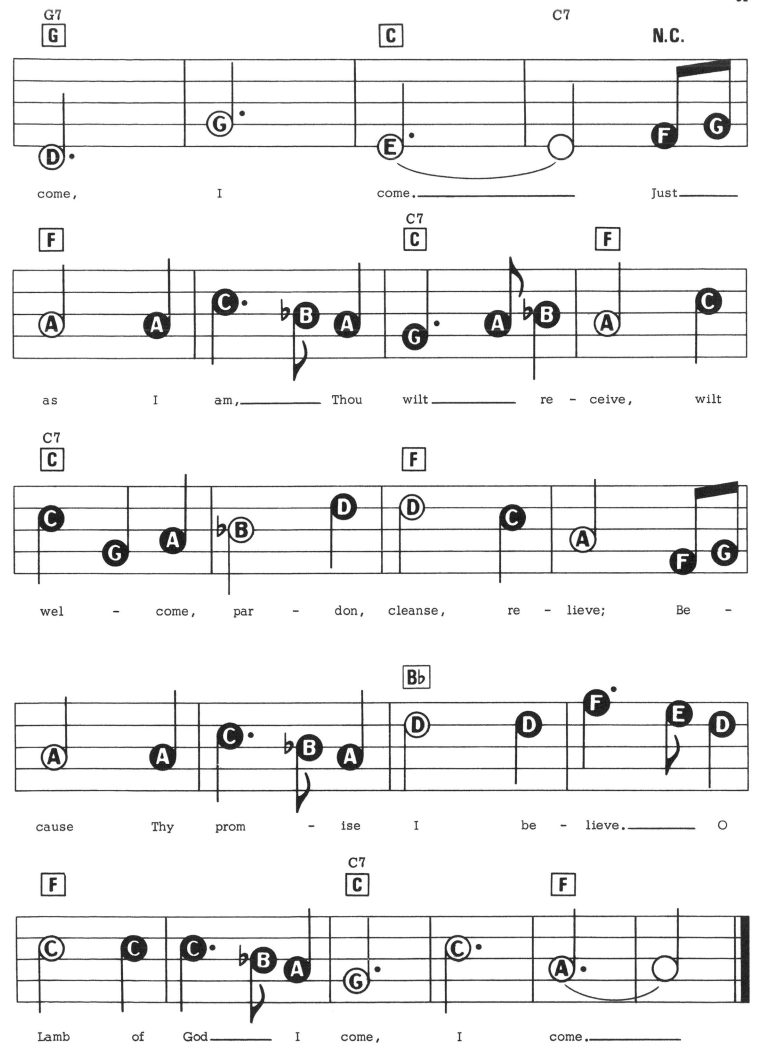

Just Over in the Gloryland

Registration 1
Rhythm: Ballad or Fox Trot

Words and Music by J.W. Acuff
and Emmett Dean

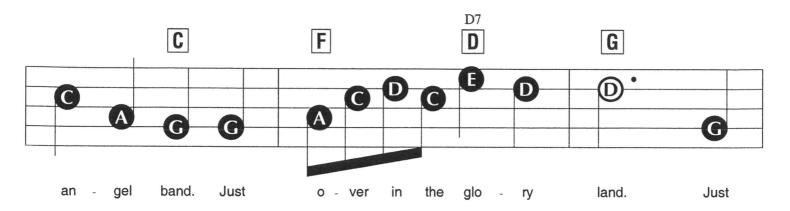

an - gel band. Just o - ver in the glo - ry land. Just

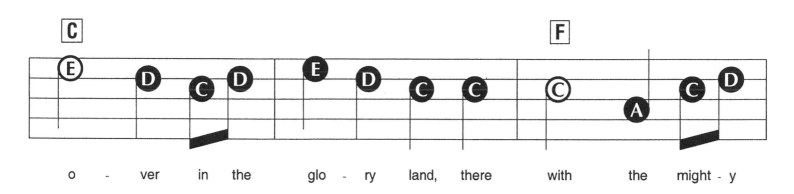

o - ver in the glo - ry land, there with the might - y

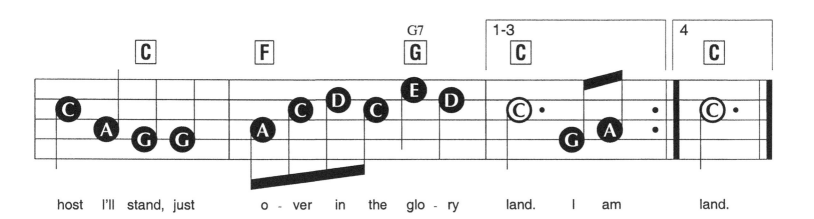

host I'll stand, just o - ver in the glo - ry land. I am land.

Additional Lyrics

3. What a joyful tho't that my Lord I'll see,
   Just over in the glory land;
   And with kindred saved there forever be,
   Just over in the glory land.
   Refrain

4. With the blood-washed throng I will shout and sing,
   Just over in the glory land;
   Glad hosannas to Christ, the Lord and King,
   Just over in the glory land.
   Refrain

The Lily of the Valley

Registration 6
Rhythm: Ballad

Words by Charles W. Fry
Music by William S. Hays

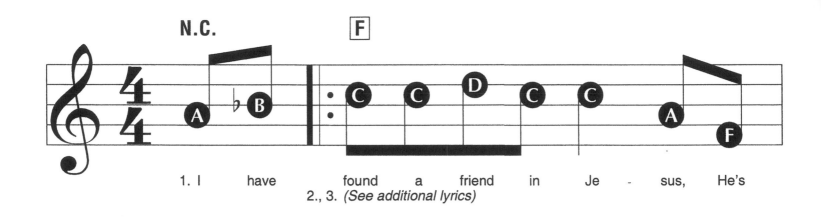

1. I have found a friend in Je - sus, He's
2., 3. *(See additional lyrics)*

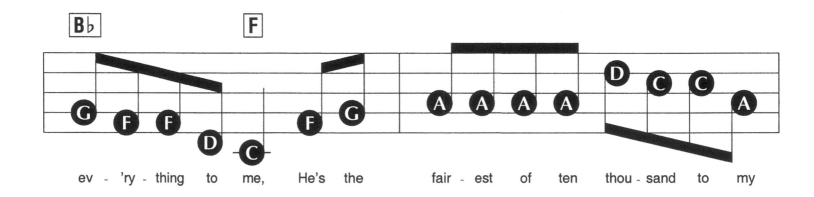

ev - 'ry - thing to me, He's the fair - est of ten thou - sand to my

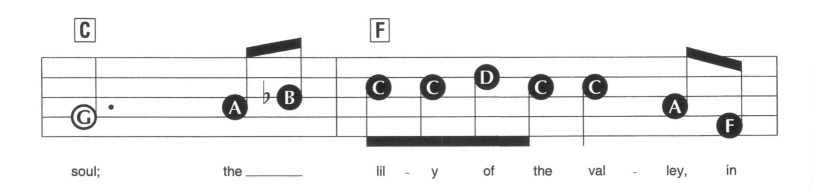

soul; the _____ lil - y of the val - ley, in

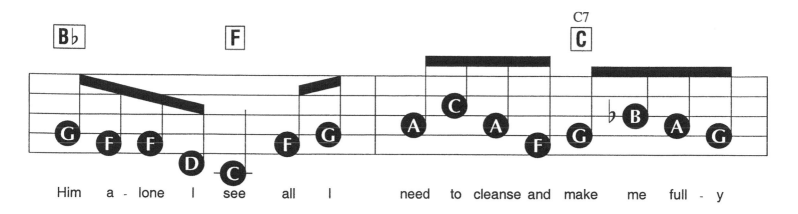

Him a - lone I see all I need to cleanse and make me full - y

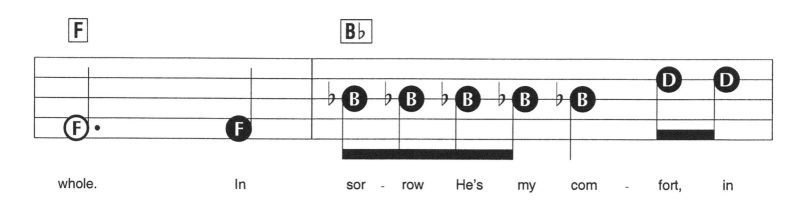

whole. In sor - row He's my com - fort, in

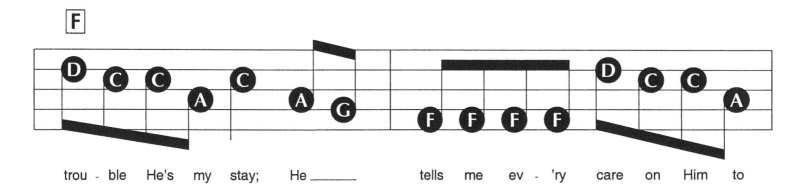

trou - ble He's my stay; He tells me ev - 'ry care on Him to

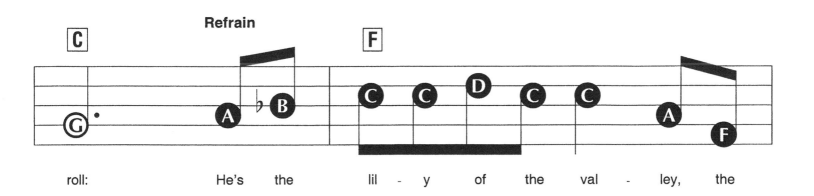

roll: He's the lil - y of the val - ley, the

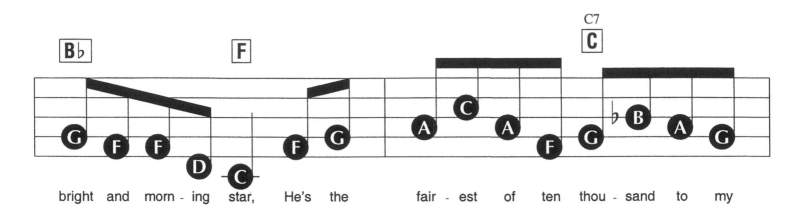

bright and morn - ing star, He's the fair - est of ten thou - sand to my

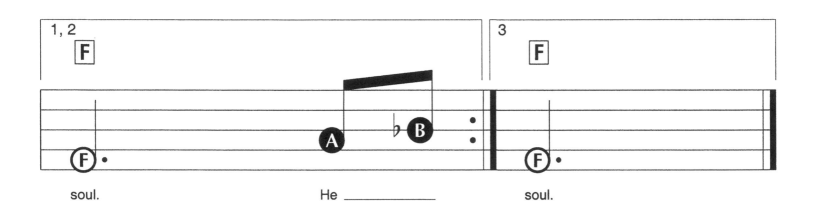

soul.

He _____

soul.

Additional Lyrics

2. He all my grief has taken, and all my sorrows borne;
In temptation He's my strong and mighty tow'r;
I have all for him forsaken, and all my idols torn
From my heart and now He keeps me by His pow'r.
Though all the world forsake me, and Satan tempt me sore,
Through Jesus I shall safely reach the goal:
Refrain

3. He will never, never leave me, nor yet forsake me here,
While I live by faith and do His blessed will;
A wall of fire about me, I've nothing now to fear,
With His manna He my hungry soul shall fill.
Then sweeping up to glory to see His blessed face,
Where rivers of delight shall ever roll:
Refrain

Send the Light

Registration 3
Rhythm: $\frac{6}{8}$ March

Words and Music by
Charles Gabriel

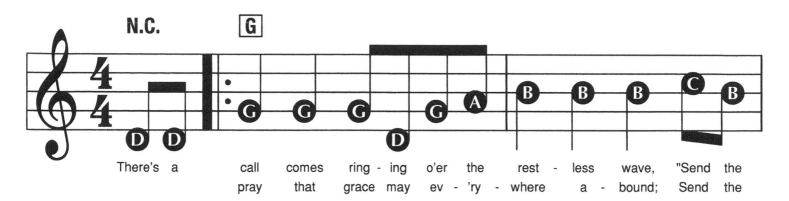

There's a / call comes ring-ing o'er the rest-less wave, "Send the
pray that / grace may ev-'ry-where a-bound; Send the

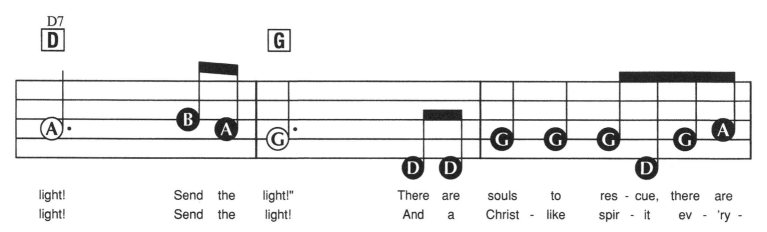

light! / Send the light!" There are souls to res-cue, there are
light! / Send the light! And a Christ-like spir-it ev-'ry-

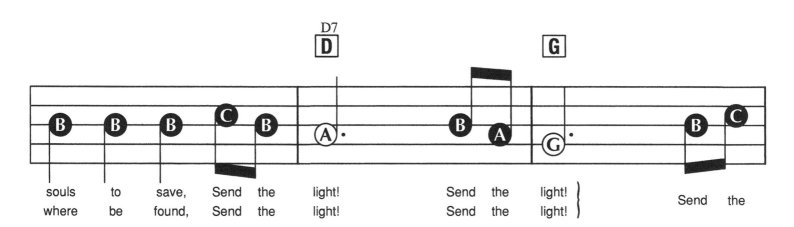

souls to save, Send the light! Send the light!
where be found, Send the light! Send the light! Send the

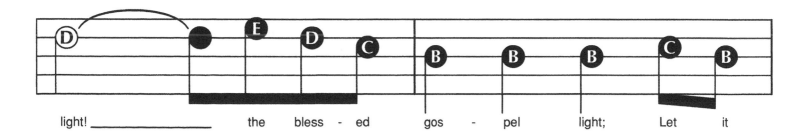

light! _____ the bless-ed gos-pel light; Let it

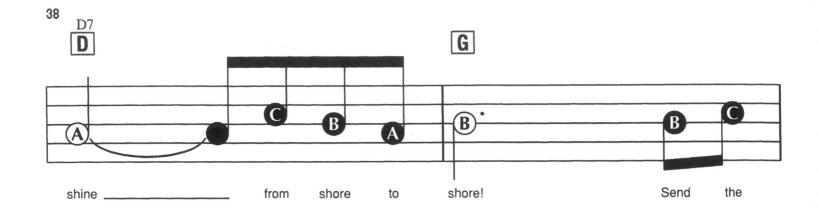

shine _____ from shore to shore! Send the

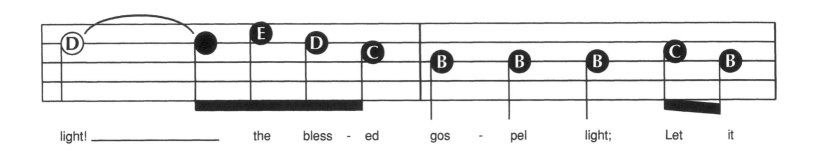

light! _____ the bless - ed gos - pel light; Let it

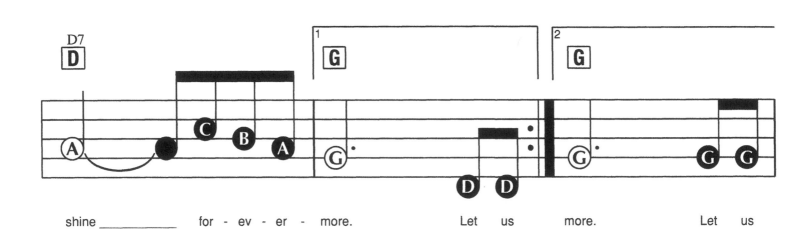

shine _____ for - ev - er - more. Let us more. Let us

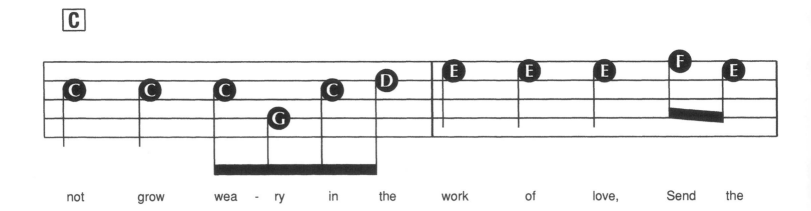

not grow wea - ry in the work of love, Send the

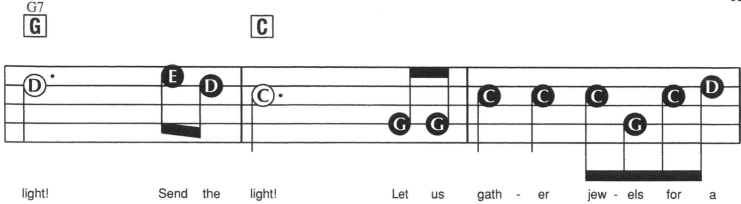

light! Send the light! Let us gath-er jew-els for a

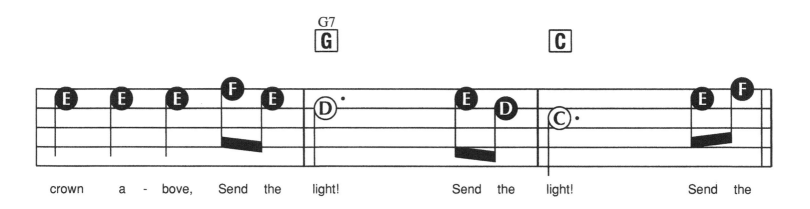

crown a - bove, Send the light! Send the light! Send the

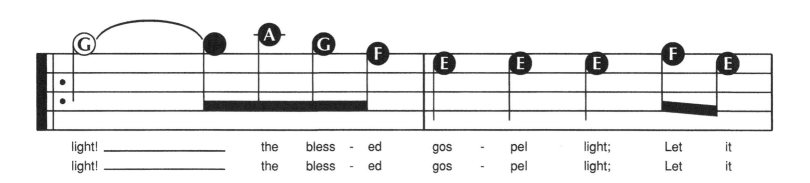

light! _____ the bless - ed gos - pel light; Let it
light! _____ the bless - ed gos - pel light; Let it

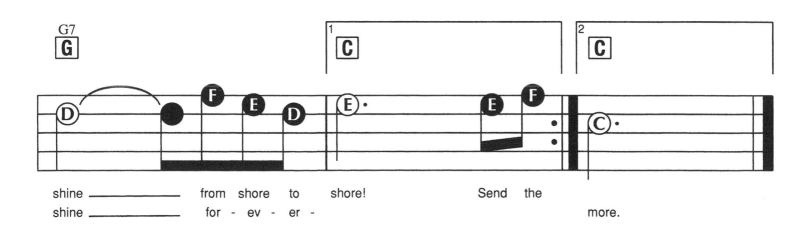

shine _____ from shore to shore! Send the
shine _____ for - ev - er - more.

Near the Cross

Registration 6
Rhythm: Waltz

Words by Fanny Crosby
Music by William H. Doane

Refrain

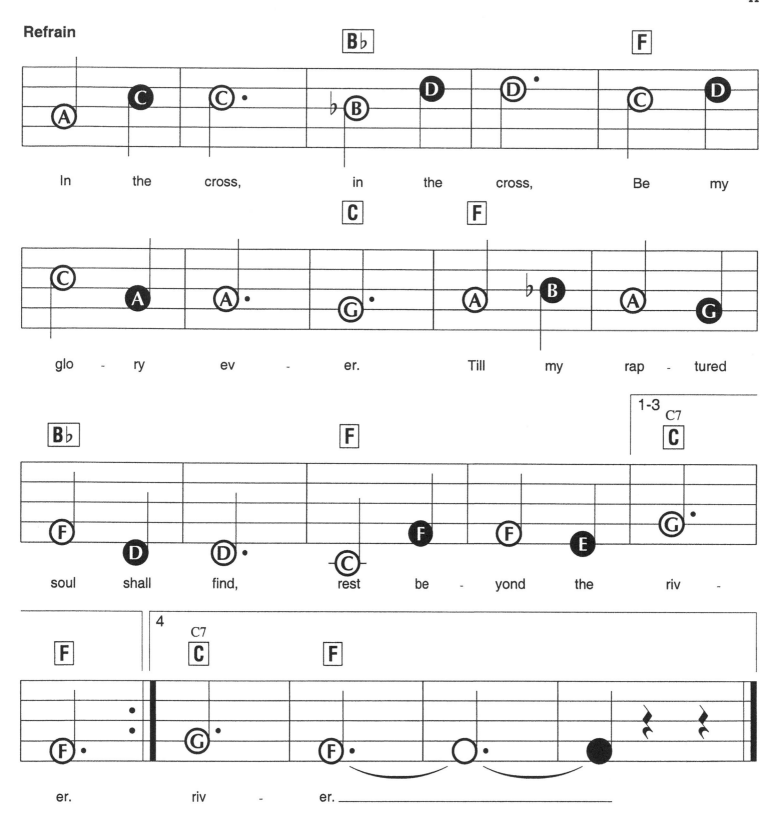

Additional Lyrics

3. Near the cross! O Lamb of God,
   Bring its scenes before me;
   Help me walk from day to day,
   With its shadows o'er me.
   Refrain

4. Near the cross I'll watch and wait,
   Hoping, trusting ever,
   Till I reach the golden strand,
   Just beyond the river.
   Refrain

Nothing but the Blood

Registration 2
Rhythm: Ballad or Fox Trot

Words and Music by
Robert Lowry

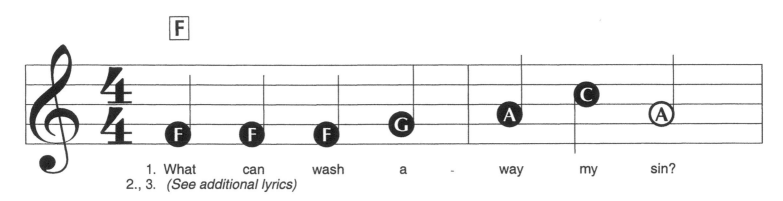

1. What can wash a - way my sin?
2., 3. *(See additional lyrics)*

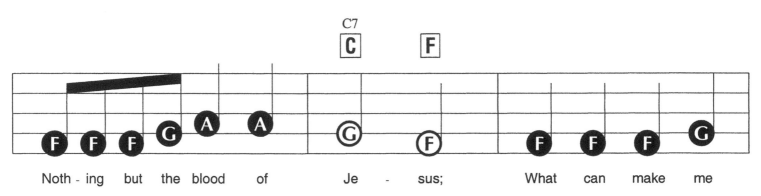

Noth - ing but the blood of Je - sus; What can make me

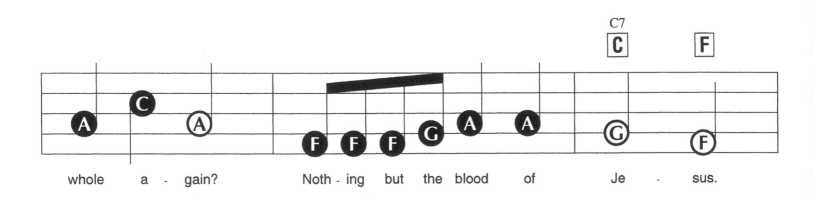

whole a - gain? Noth - ing but the blood of Je - sus.

Refrain

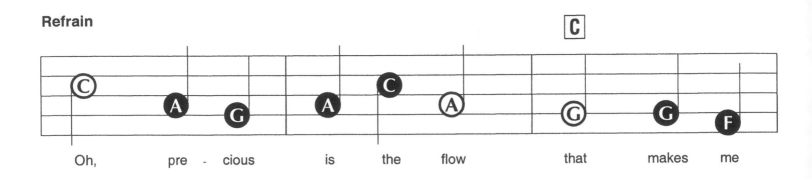

Oh, pre - cious is the flow that makes me

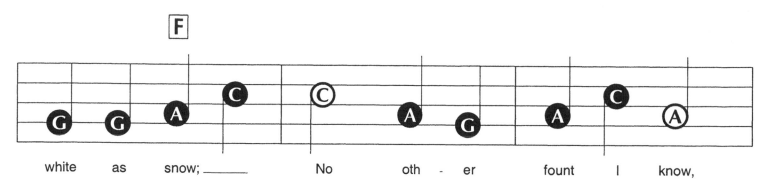

white   as   snow; _____   No   oth - er   fount   I   know,

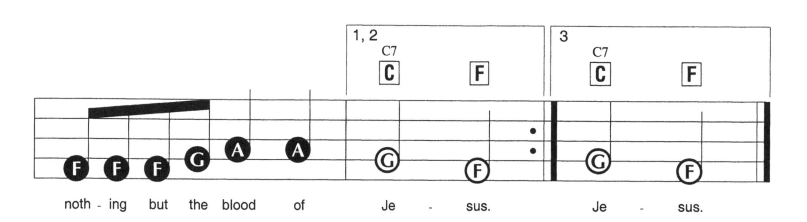

noth - ing   but   the   blood   of   Je - sus.   Je - sus.

Additional Lyrics

2. For my pardon this I see
   Nothing but the blood of Jesus;
   For my cleansing this my plea
   Nothing but the blood of Jesus.
   Refrain

3. Nothing can for sin atone
   Nothing but the blood of Jesus;
   Naught of good that I have done
   Nothing but the blood of Jesus.
   Refrain

The Old Rugged Cross

Registration 2
Rhythm: Waltz

By Rev. George Bennard

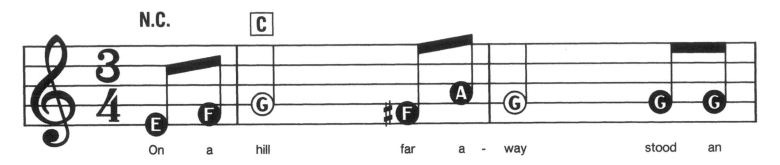

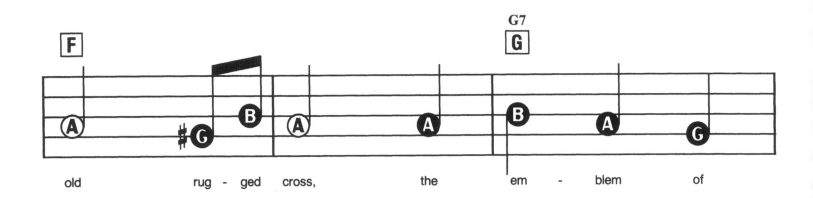

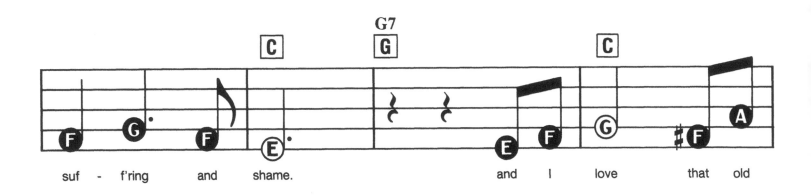

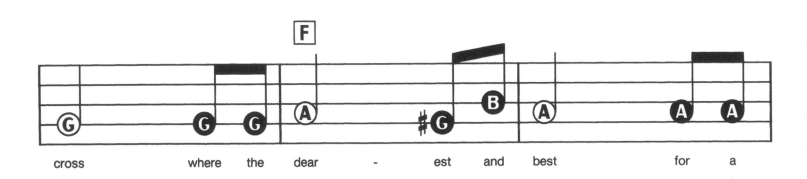

45

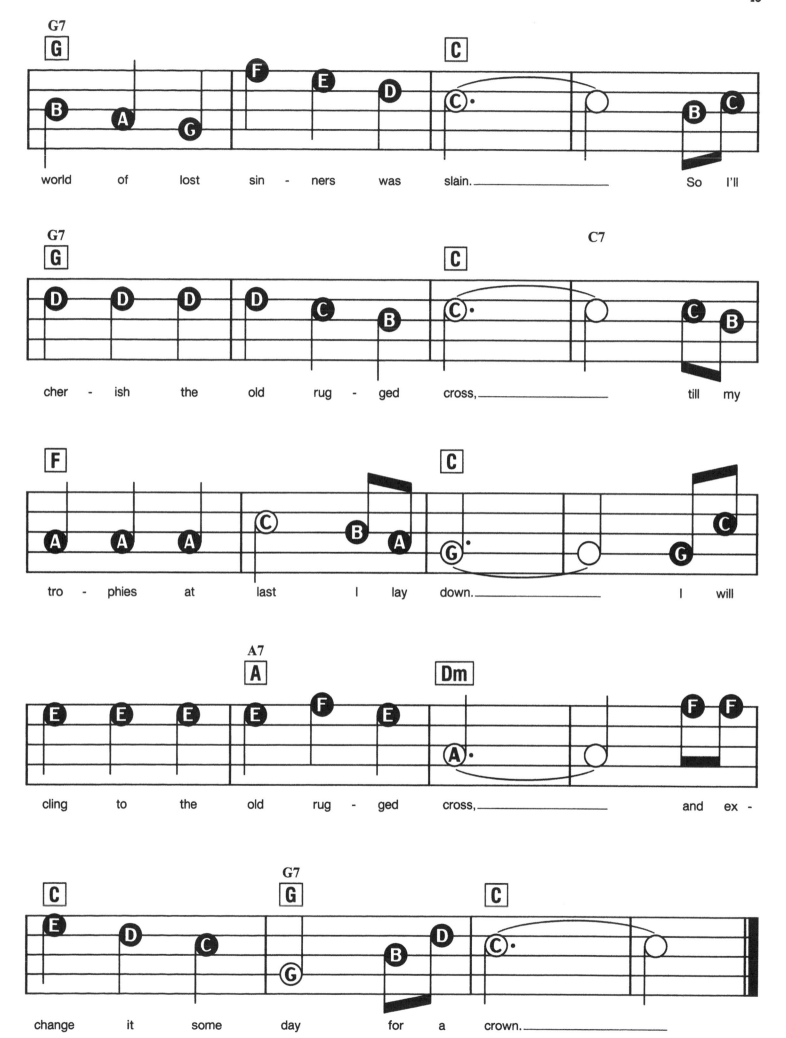

Pass Me Not, O Gentle Savior

Registration 5
Rhythm: Ballad or Fox Trot

Words by Fanny J. Crosby
Music by William H. Doane

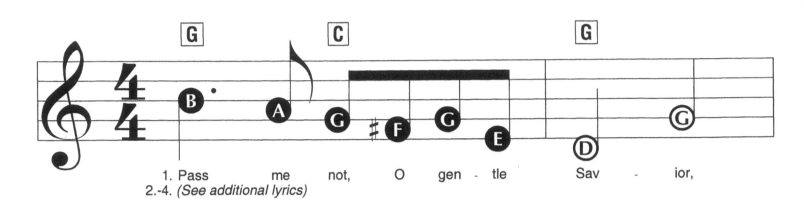

1. Pass me not, O gen - tle Sav - ior,
2.-4. *(See additional lyrics)*

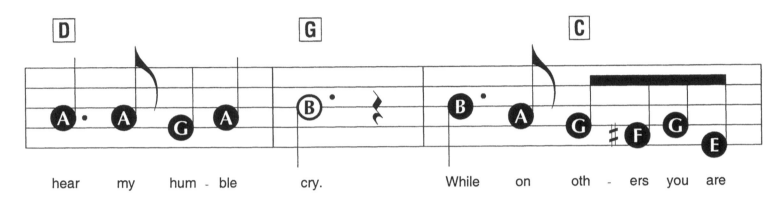

hear my hum - ble cry. While on oth - ers you are

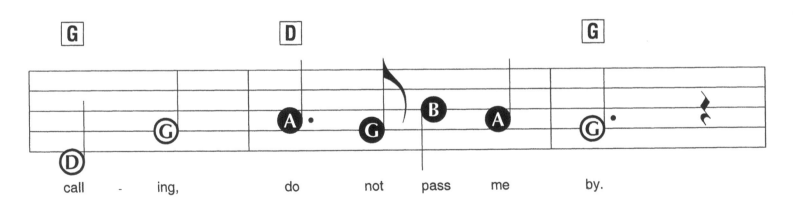

call - ing, do not pass me by.

Refrain

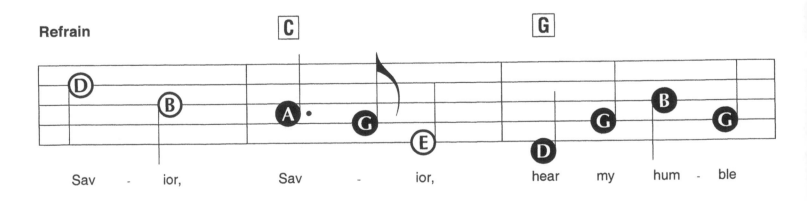

Sav - ior, Sav - ior, hear my hum - ble

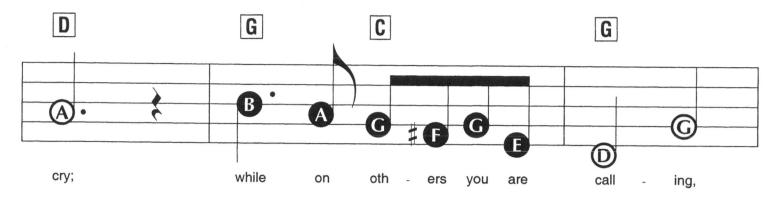

cry;   while   on   oth - ers you are   call - ing,

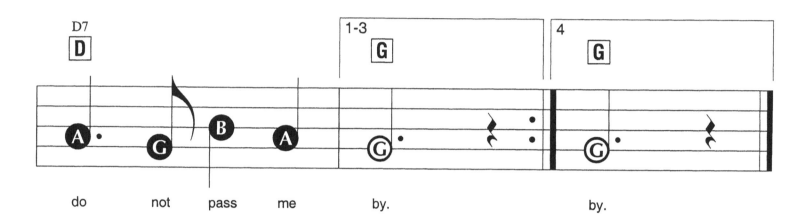

do   not   pass   me   by.   by.

Additional Lyrics

2. Let me at your throne of mercy find a sweet relief;
   Kneeling there in deep contrition, help my unbelief.
   Refrain

3. Trusting only in your merit, would I seek your face;
   Heal my wounded, broken spirit, save me by your grace.
   Refrain

4. Be the Spring of all my comfort, more than life to me;
   Not just here on earth beside me, but eternally.
   Refrain

Power in the Blood

Registration 5
Rhythm: Fox Trot

Traditional

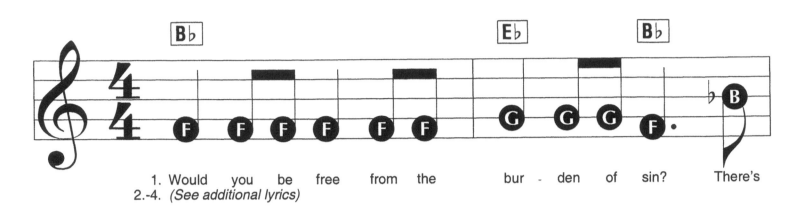

1. Would you be free from the bur - den of sin? There's
2.-4. (See additional lyrics)

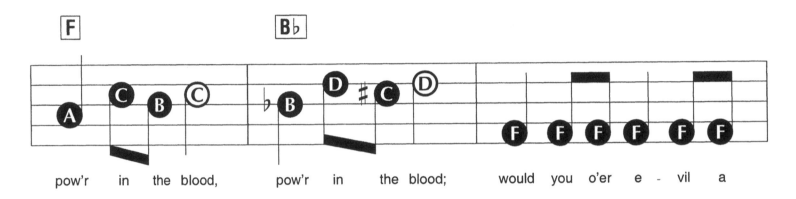

pow'r in the blood, pow'r in the blood; would you o'er e - vil a

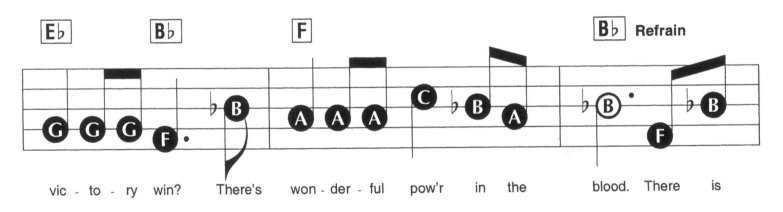

vic - to - ry win? There's won - der - ful pow'r in the blood. There is

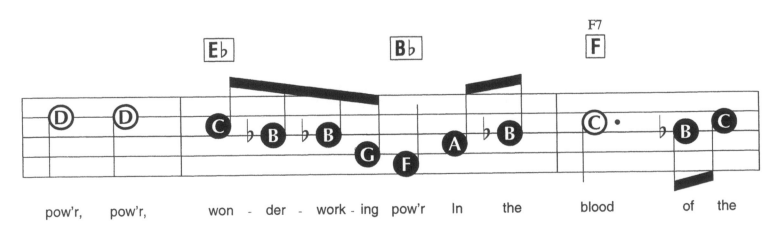

pow'r, pow'r, won - der - work - ing pow'r In the blood of the

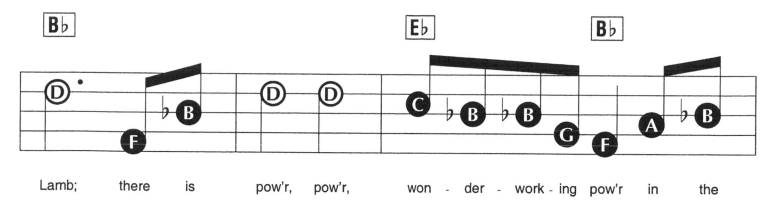

Lamb; there is pow'r, pow'r, won - der - work - ing pow'r in the

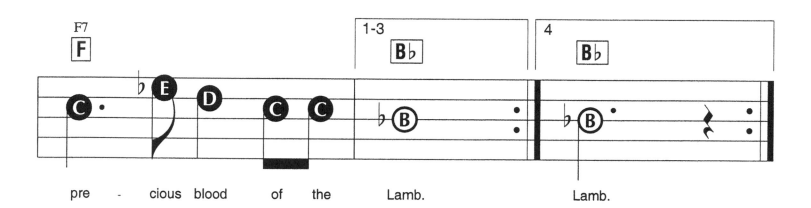

pre - cious blood of the Lamb. Lamb.

Additional Lyrics

2. Would you be free from your passion and pride?
   There's pow'r in the blood, pow'r in the blood;
   Come for a cleansing to Calvary's tide;
   There's wonderful pow'r in the blood.
   Refrain

3. Would you be whiter, much whiter than snow?
   There's pow'r in the blood, pow'r in the blood;
   Sin stains are lost in its lifegiving flow;
   There's wonderful pow'r in the blood.
   Refrain

4. Would you do service for Jesus your King?
   There's pow'r in the blood, pow'r in the blood;
   Would you live daily His praises to sing?
   There's wonderful pow'r in the blood.
   Refrain

Rock of Ages

Registration 6
Rhythm: Waltz

Text by Augustus M. Toplady
Music by Thomas Hastings

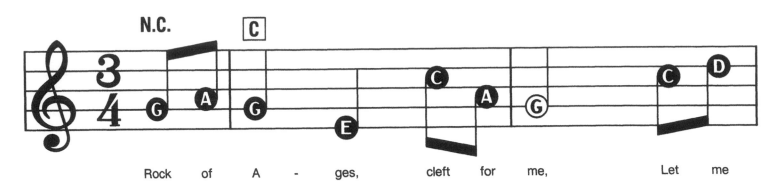

Rock of A - ges, cleft for me, Let me

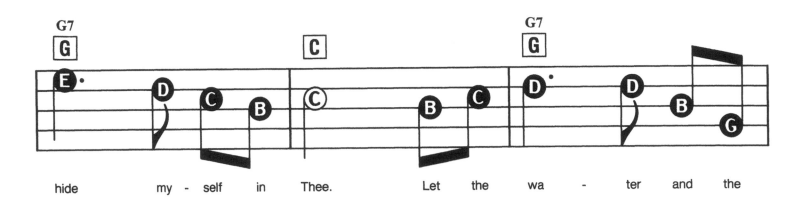

hide my - self in Thee. Let the wa - ter and the

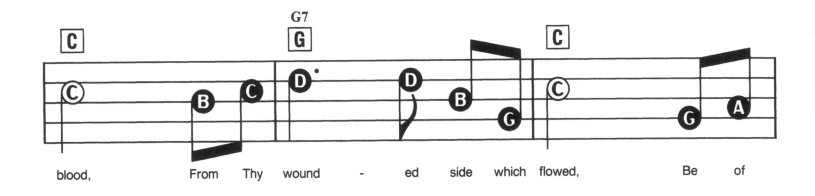

blood, From Thy wound - ed side which flowed, Be of

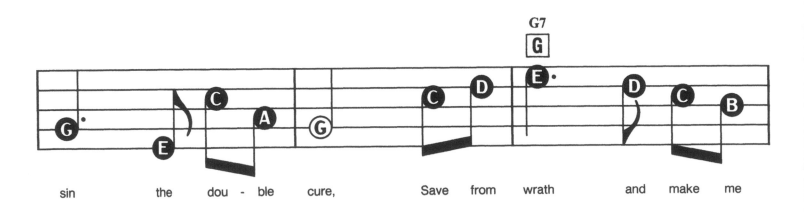

sin the dou - ble cure, Save from wrath and make me

51

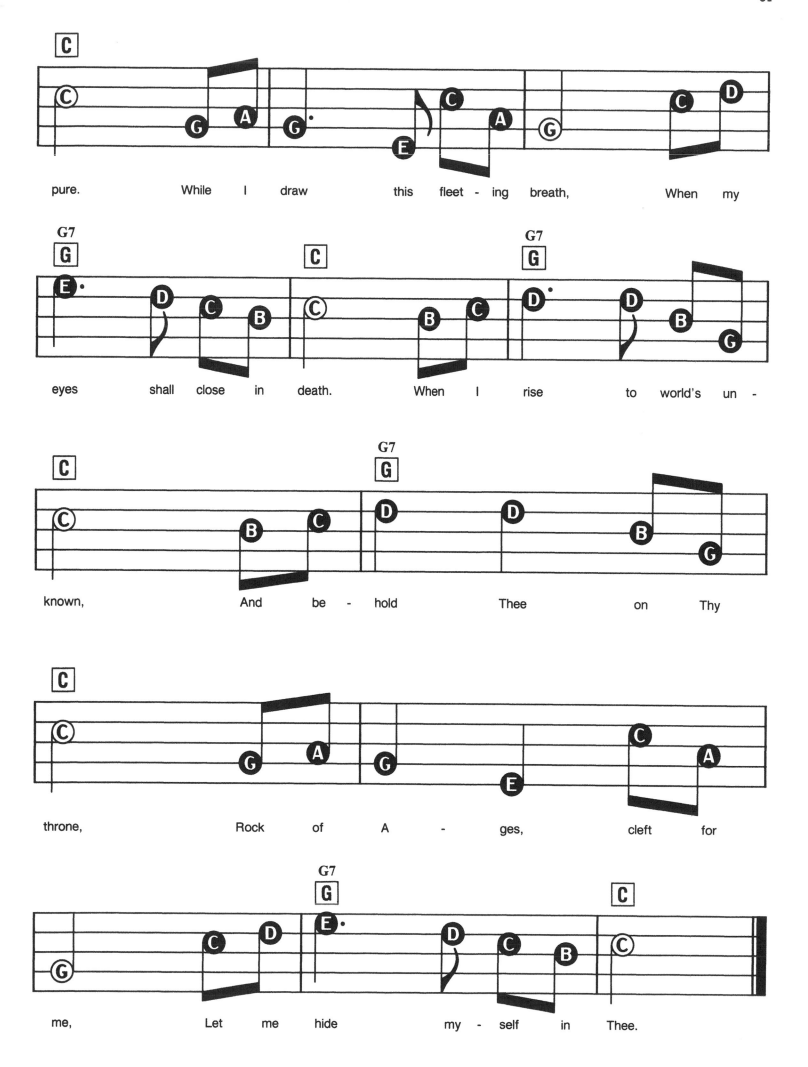

Shall We Gather at the River?

Registration 6
Rhythm: March

Words and Music by
Robert Lowry

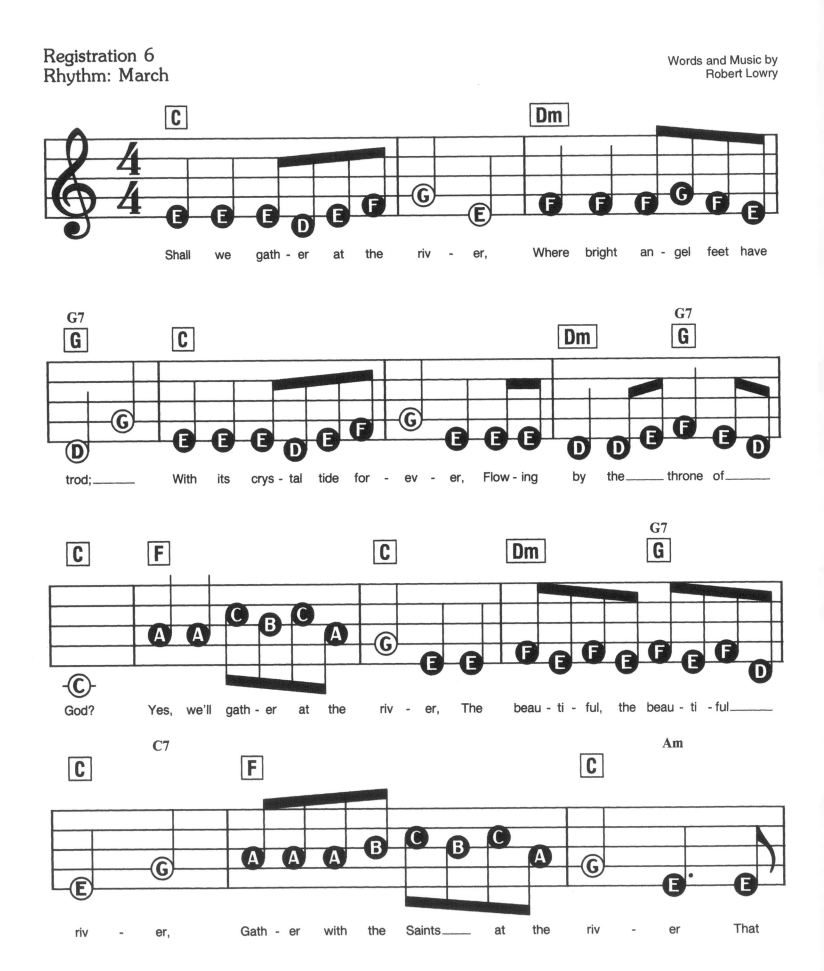

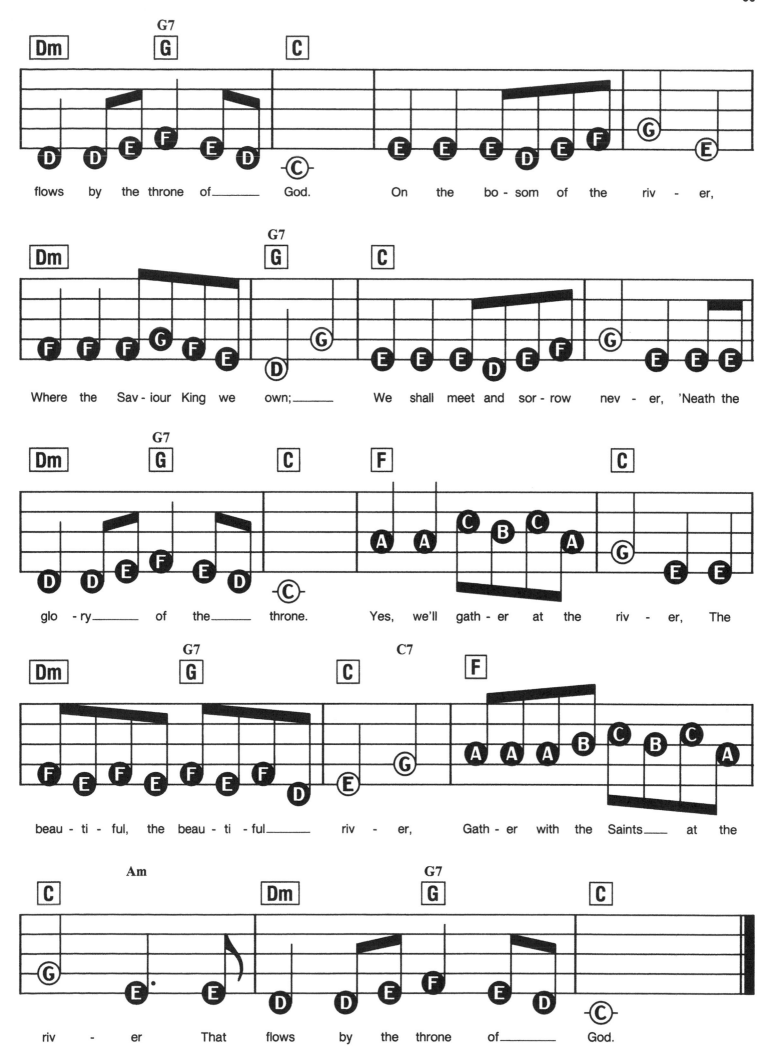

Since Jesus Came into My Heart

Registration 5
Rhythm: Rock or 8 Beat

Words by R.H. McDaniel
Music by Charles H. Gabriel

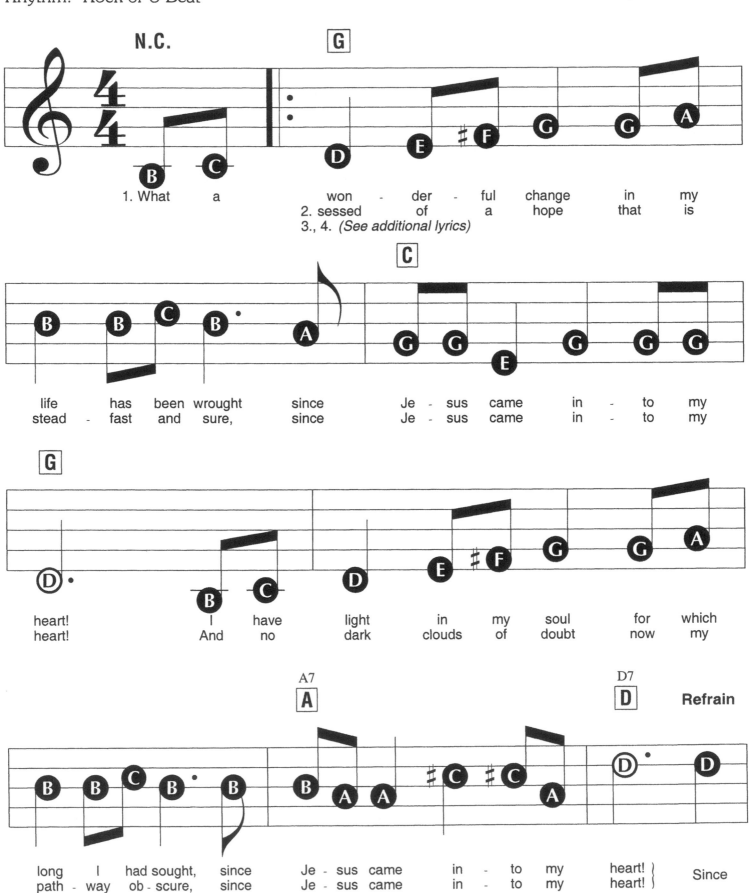

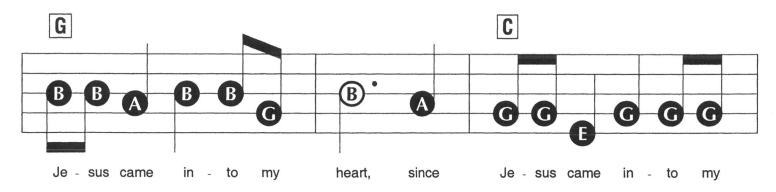

Je - sus came in - to my heart, since Je - sus came in - to my

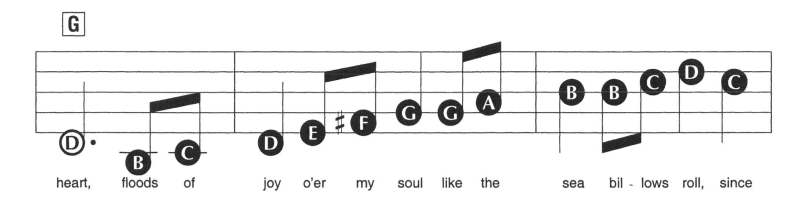

heart, floods of joy o'er my soul like the sea bil - lows roll, since

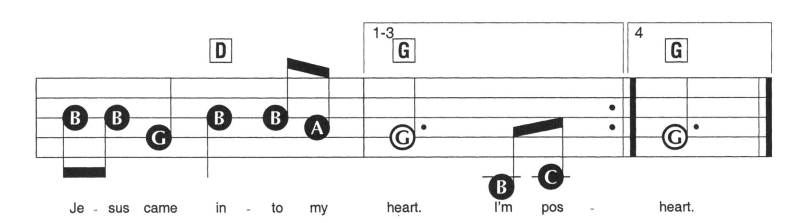

Je - sus came in - to my heart. I'm pos - heart.

Additional Lyrics

3. There's a light in the valley of death now for me,
   Since Jesus came into my heart!
   And the gates of the city beyond I can see,
   Since Jesus came into my heart!
   Refrain

4. I shall go there to dwell in that city, I know,
   Since Jesus came into my heart!
   And I'm happy, so happy, as onward I go,
   Since Jesus came into my heart!
   Refrain

Softly and Tenderly

Registration 2
No Rhythm

Words and Music by
Will L. Thompson

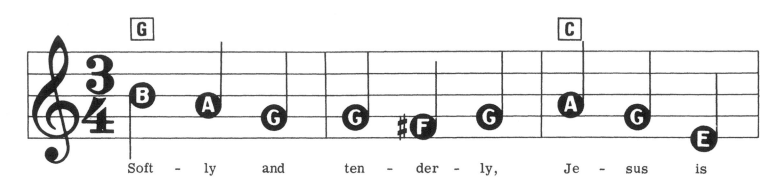

Soft - ly and ten - der - ly, Je - sus is

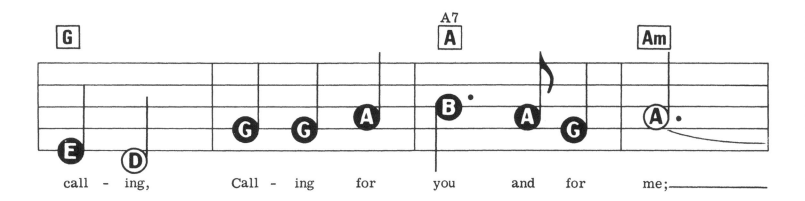

call - ing, Call - ing for you and for me;_____

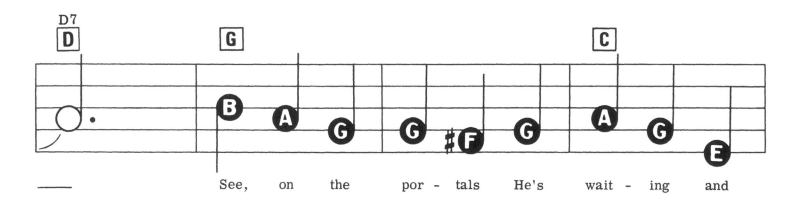

_____ See, on the por - tals He's wait - ing and

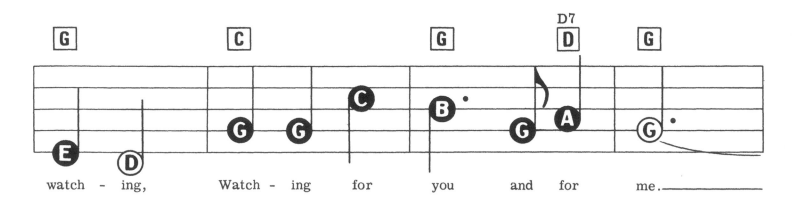

watch - ing, Watch - ing for you and for me._____

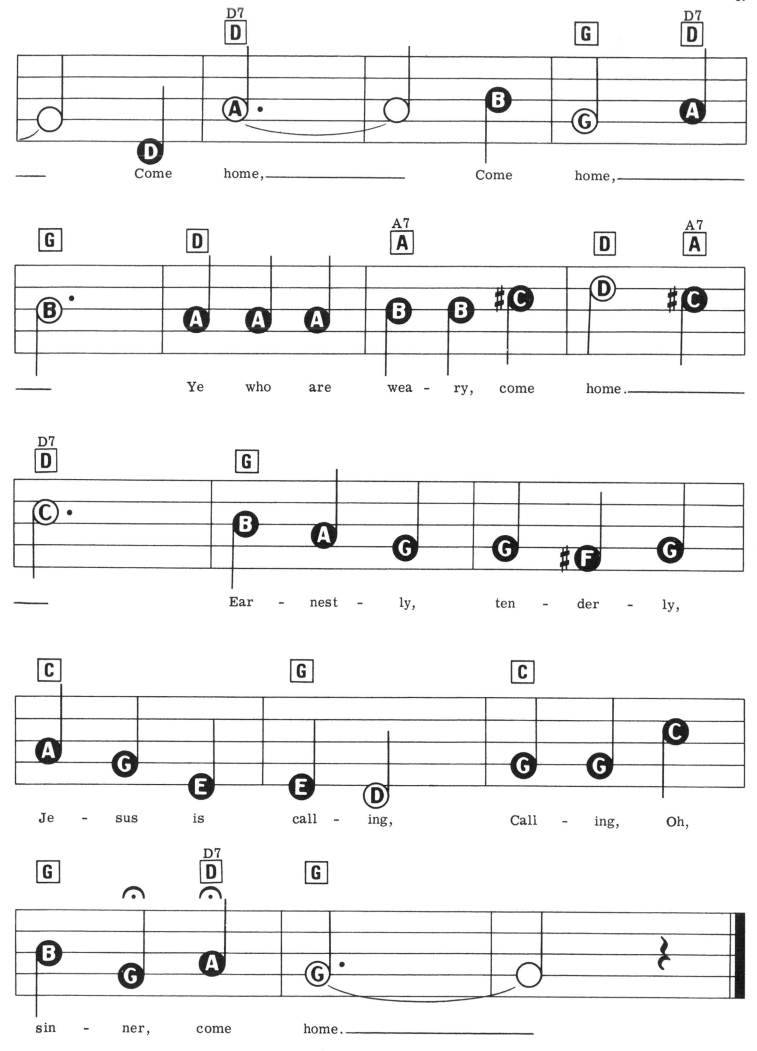

Standing on the Promises

Registration 5
Rhythm: March or Swing

Words and Music by
R. Kelso Carter

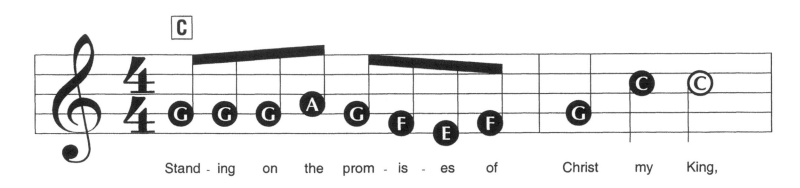

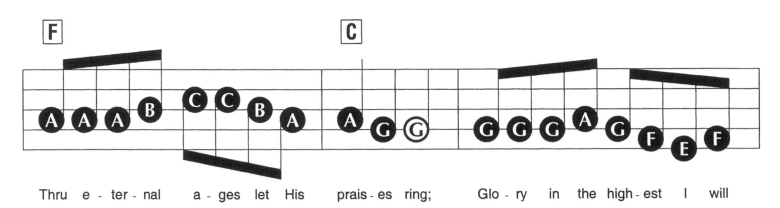

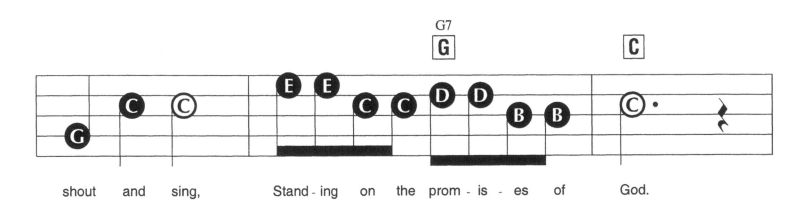

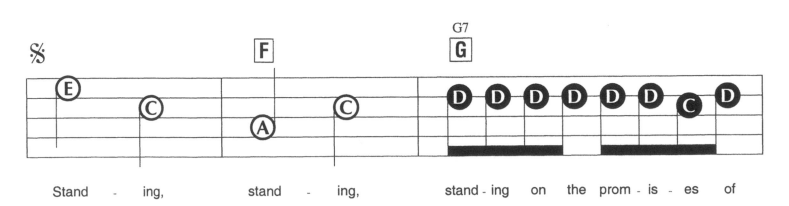

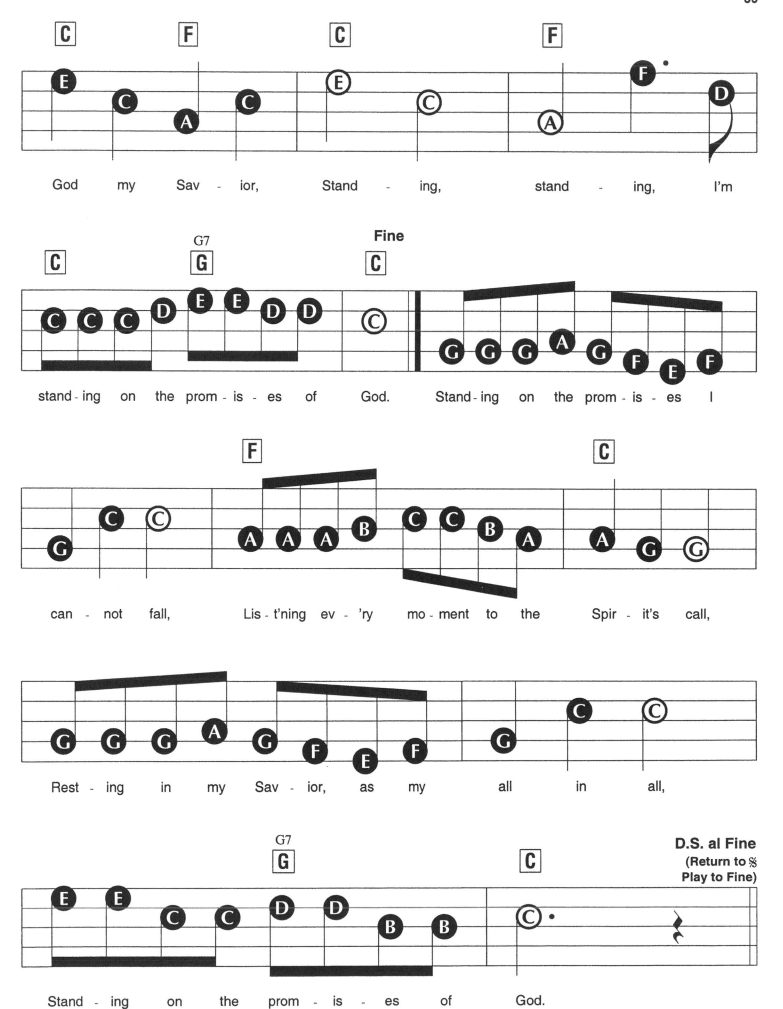

Sweet Hour of Prayer

Registration 6
Rhythm: Waltz

Words by William W. Walford
Music by William B. Bradbury

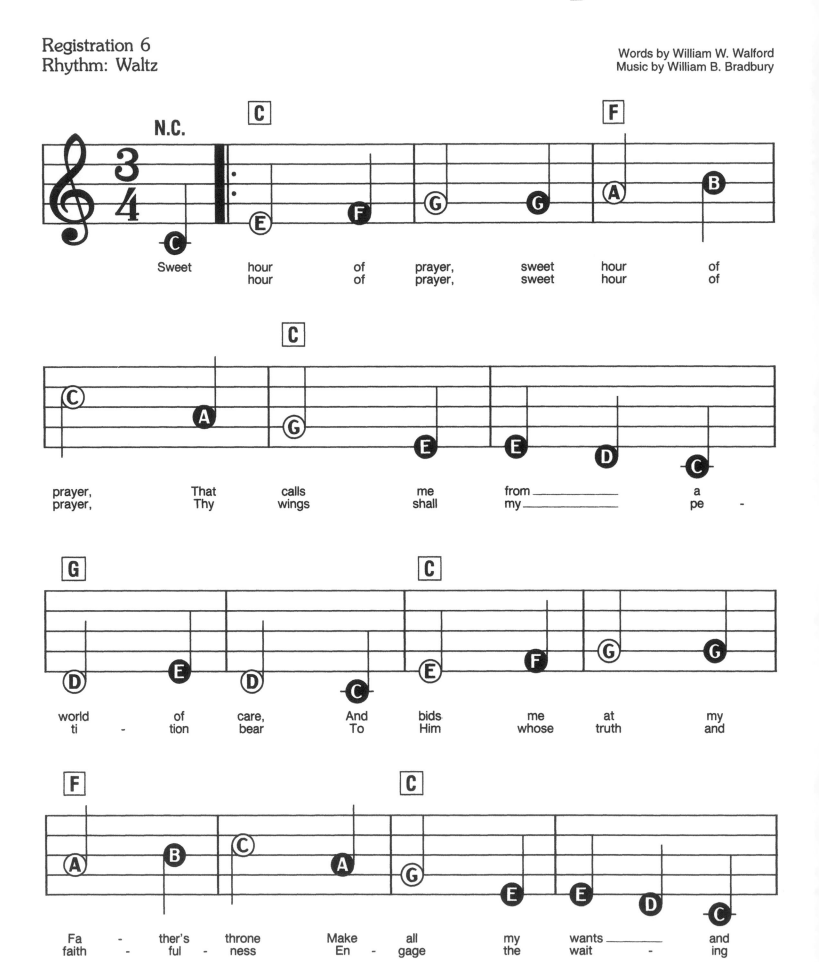

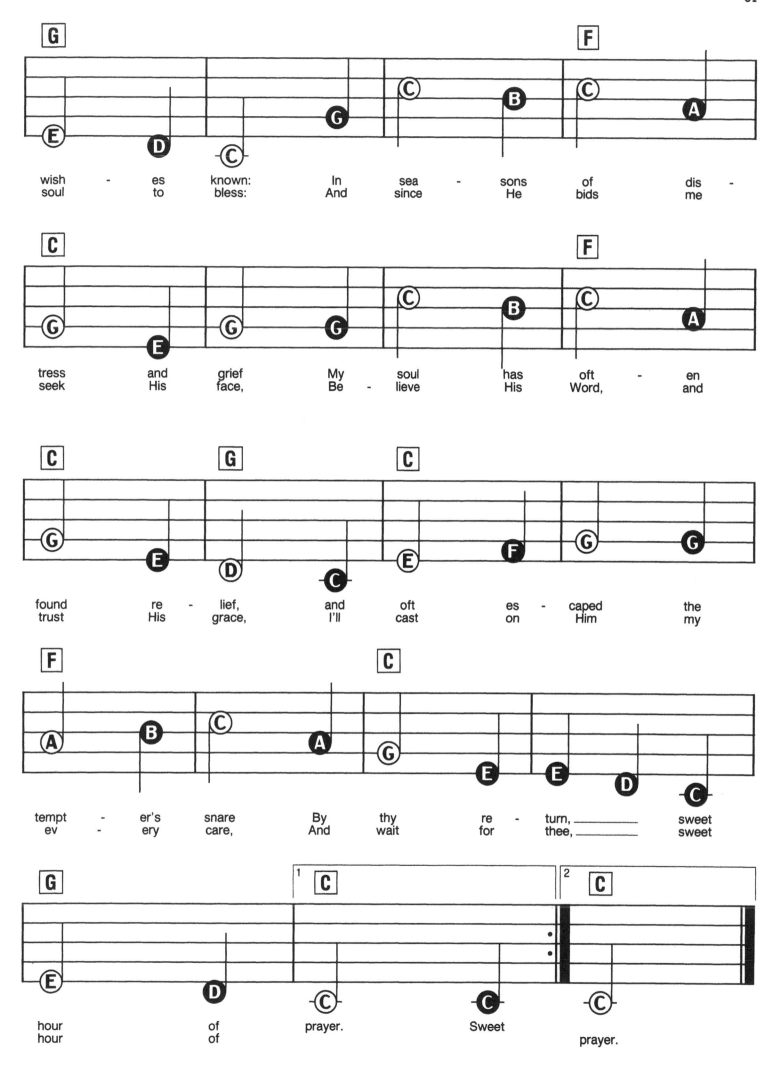

Tell It to Jesus

Registration 10
Rhythm: Ballad or Fox Trot

Traditional

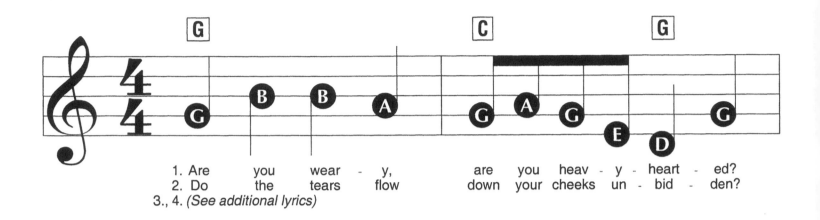

1. Are you wear - y, are you heav - y - heart - ed?
2. Do the tears flow down your cheeks un - bid - den?
3., 4. *(See additional lyrics)*

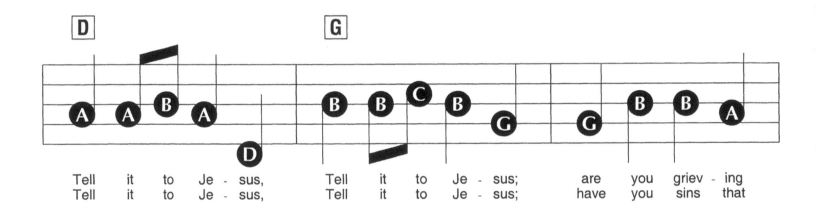

Tell it to Je - sus, Tell it to Je - sus; are you griev - ing
Tell it to Je - sus, Tell it to Je - sus; have you sins that

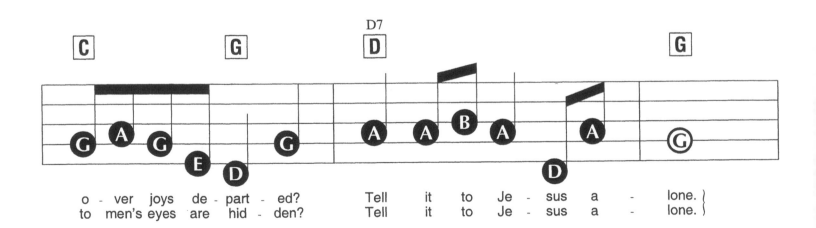

o - ver joys de - part - ed? Tell it to Je - sus a - lone.
to men's eyes are hid - den? Tell it to Je - sus a - lone.

Refrain

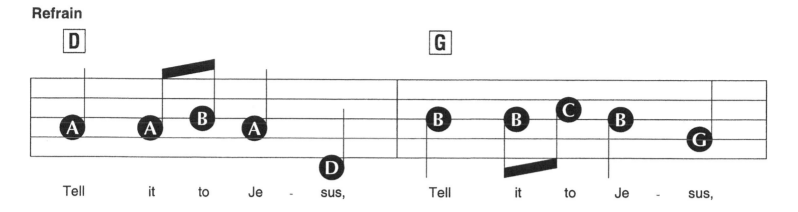

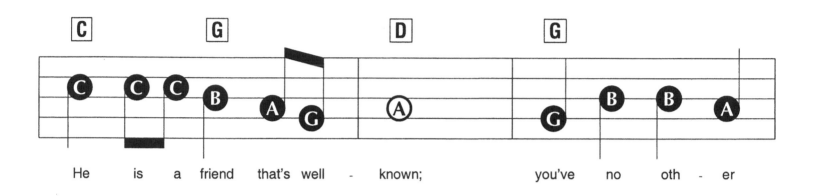

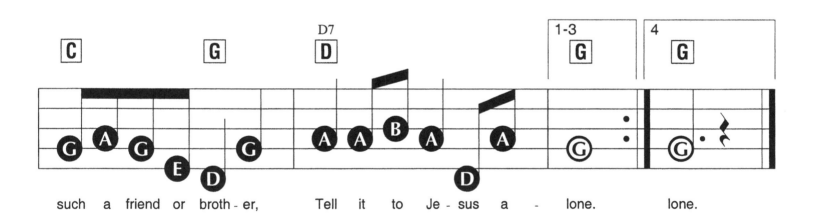

Additional Lyrics

3. Do you fear the gath'ring clouds of sorrow?
   Tell it to Jesus, Tell it to Jesus;
   Are you anxious what shall be tomorrow?
   Tell it to Jesus alone.
   Refrain

4. Are you troubled at the thought of dying?
   Tell it to Jesus, Tell it to Jesus;
   For Christ's coming kingdom are you sighing?
   Tell it to Jesus alone.
   Refrain

There Is a Fountain

Registration 8
Rhythm: Ballad or Fox Trot

Words by William Cowper
Traditional American Melody
Arranged by Lowell Mason

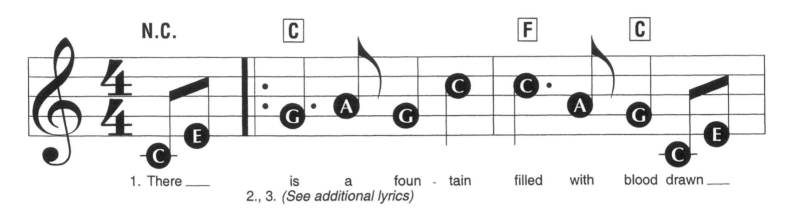

1. There _____ is a foun - tain filled with blood drawn _____
2., 3. *(See additional lyrics)*

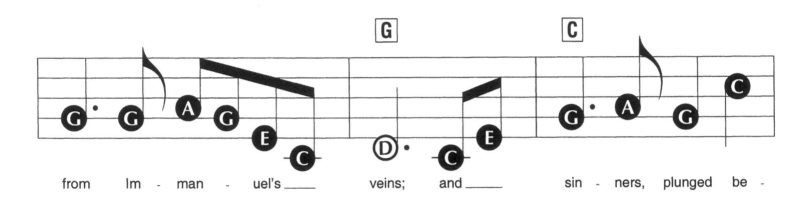

from Im - man - uel's _____ veins; and _____ sin - ners, plunged be -

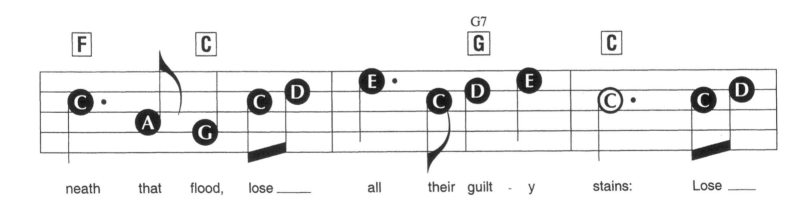

neath that flood, lose _____ all their guilt - y stains: Lose _____

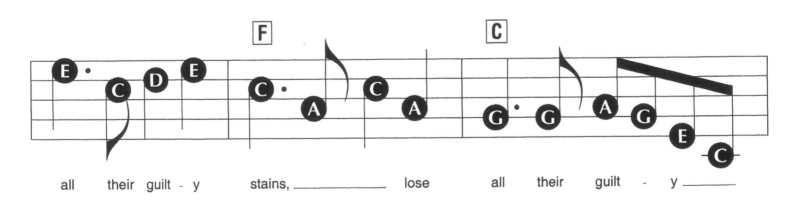

all their guilt - y stains, _____ lose all their guilt - y _____

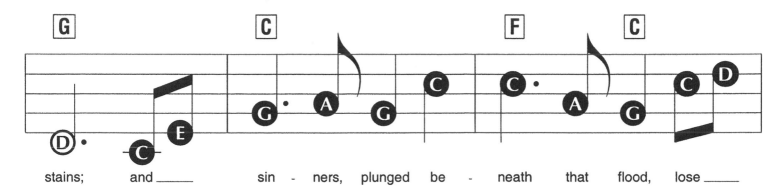

stains;   and _____   sin - ners,   plunged   be - neath   that   flood,   lose _____

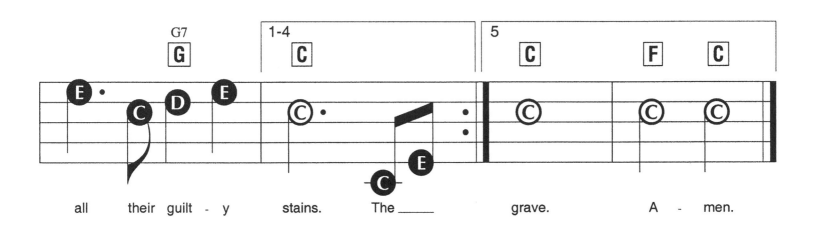

all   their   guilt - y   stains.   The _____   grave.   A - men.

Additional Lyrics

2. The dying thief rejoiced to see
   That fountain in his day;
   And there may I, though vile as he,
   Wash all my sins away:
   Wash all my sins away,
   Wash all my sins away;
   And there may I, though vile as he,
   Wash all my sins away.

3. Dear dying Lamb, Thy precious blood
   Shall never lose its power,
   Till all the ransomed Church of God
   Be saved, to sin no more:
   Be saved, to sin no more,
   Be saved, to sin no more;
   Till all the ransomed Church of God
   Be saved, to sin no more.

4. E'er since by faith, I saw the stream
   Thy flowing wounds supply,
   Redeeming love has been my theme,
   And shall be till I die:
   And shall be till I die,
   And shall be till I die;
   Redeeming love has been my theme,
   And shall be till I die.

5. Then in a nobler, sweeter song,
   I'll sing Thy power to save,
   When this poor lisping, stamm'ring tongue
   Lies silent in the grave:
   Lies silent in the grave,
   Lies silent in the grave;
   When this poor lisping, stamm'ring tongue
   Lies silent in the grave. Amen.

We'll Understand It Better By and By

Registration 6
Rhythm: Ballad or Fox Trot

Words and Music by
Charles A. Tindley

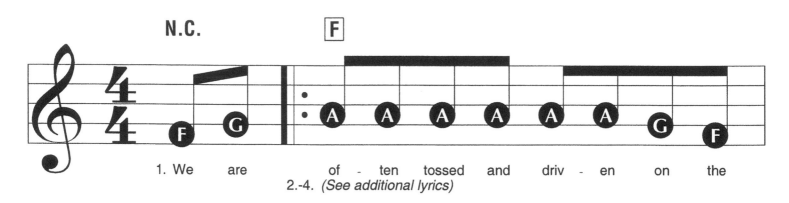

1. We are of - ten tossed and driv - en on the
2.-4. *(See additional lyrics)*

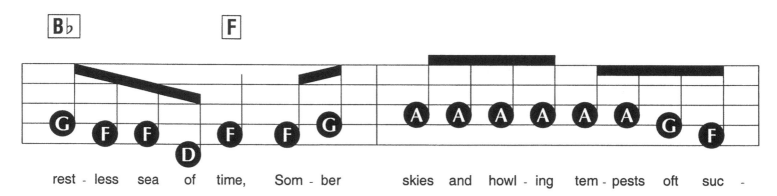

rest - less sea of time, Som - ber skies and howl - ing tem - pests oft suc -

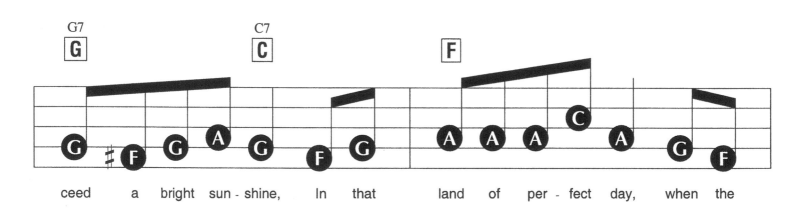

ceed a bright sun - shine, In that land of per - fect day, when the

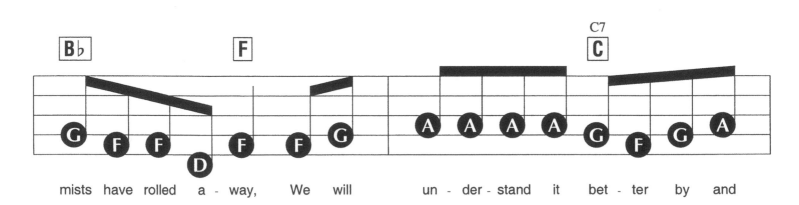

mists have rolled a - way, We will un - der - stand it bet - ter by and

Refrain

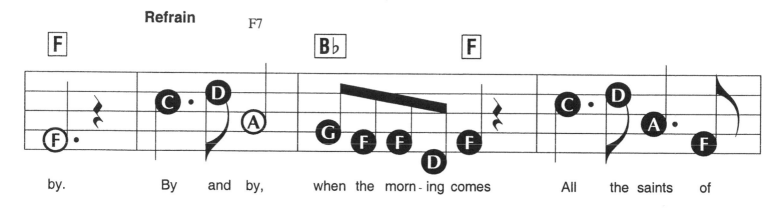

by.   By   and by,   when the morn - ing comes   All   the saints of

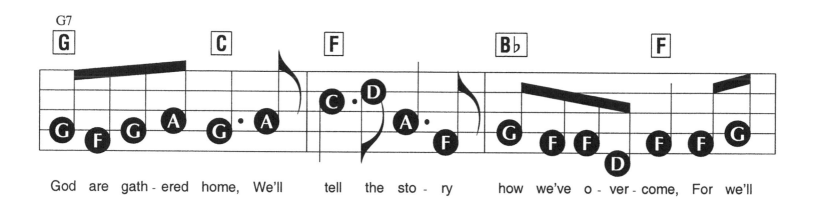

God are gath - ered home, We'll   tell   the sto - ry   how we've o - ver - come, For we'll

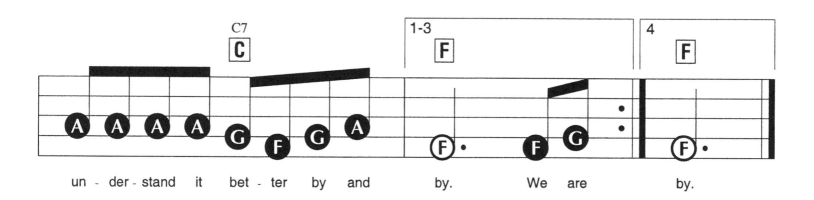

un - der - stand it bet - ter by and   by.   We are   by.

Additional Lyrics

2. We are often destitute of the things that life demands,
   Want of food and want of shelter, thirsty hills and barren lands,
   We are trusting in the Lord, and according to His word,
   We will understand it better by and by.
   Refrain

3. Trials dark on every hand, and we cannot understand,
   All the ways of God would lead us to that blessed Promised Land;
   But He guides us with His eye and we'll follow till we die,
   For we'll understand it better by and by.
   Refrain

4. Temptations, hidden snares often take us unawares,
   And our hearts are made to bleed for a thoughtless word or deed,
   And we wonder why the test when we try to do our best,
   But we'll understand it better by and by.
   Refrain

We're Marching to Zion

Registration 4
Rhythm: Waltz

Words by Isaac Watts
Music by Robert Lowry

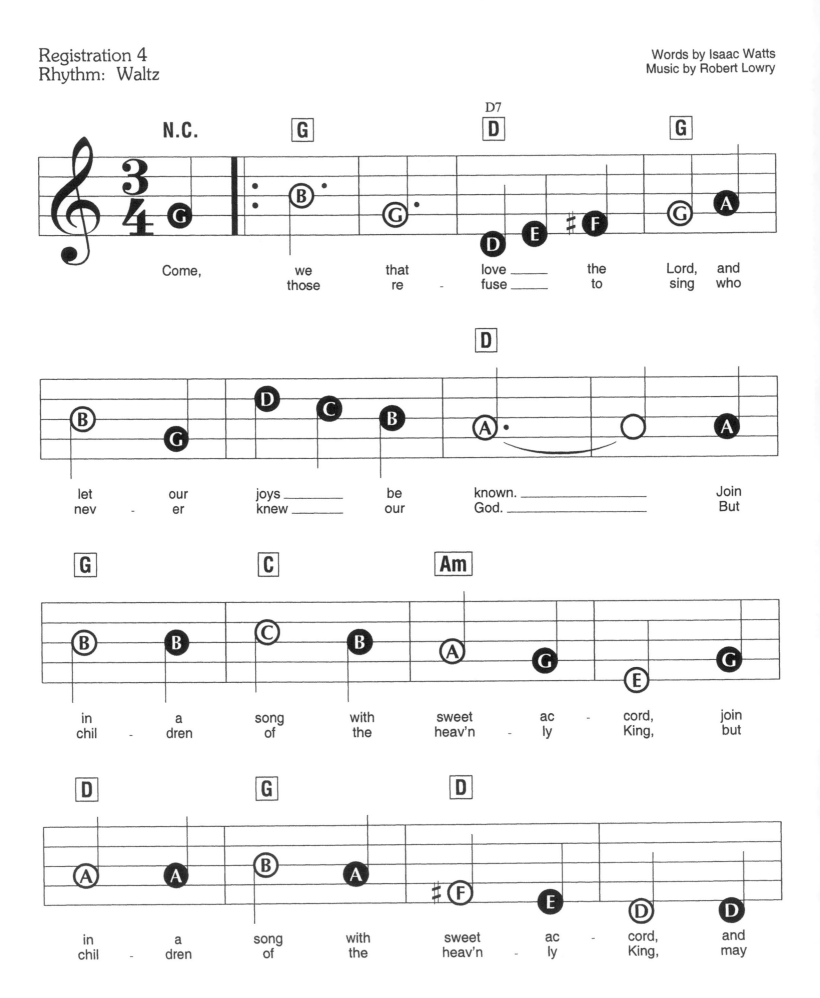

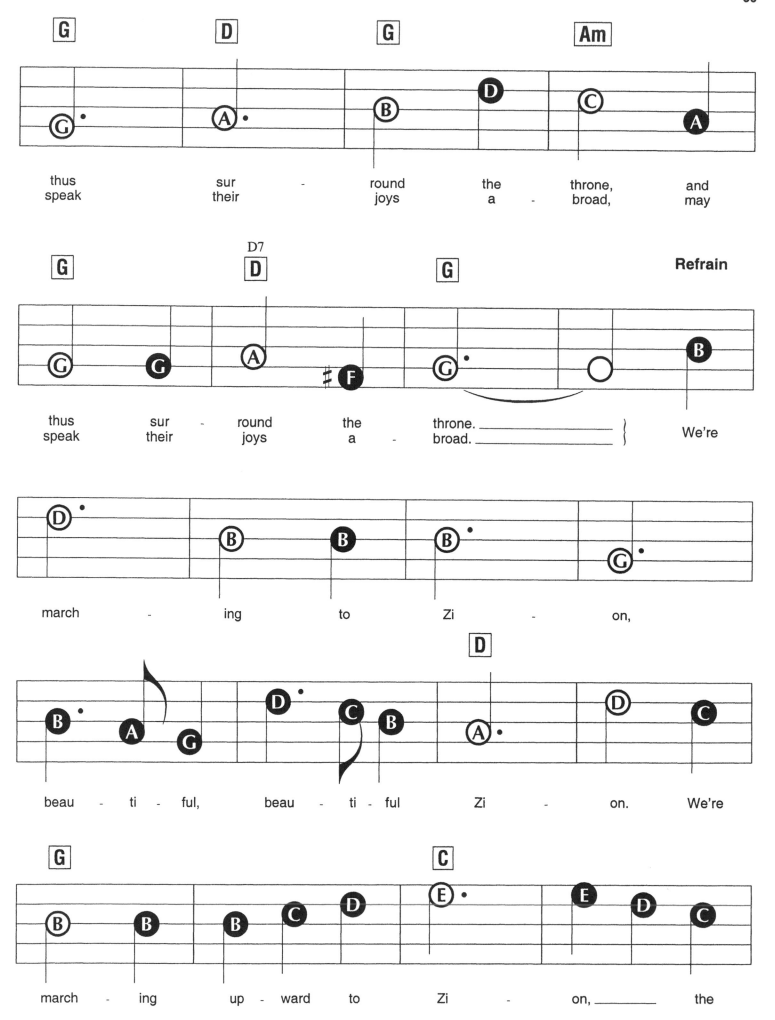

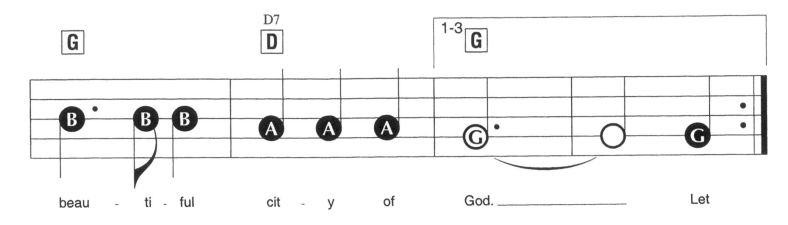

beau - ti - ful cit - y of God. _____ Let

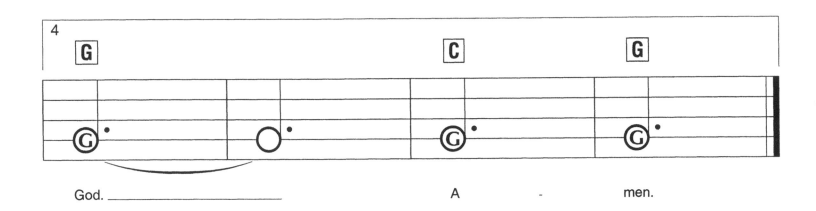

God. _____ A - men.

Additional Lyrics

3. The hill of Zion yields
   A thousand sacred sweets,
   Before we reach the heav'nly fields,
   Before we reach the heav'nly fields,
   Or walk the golden streets,
   Or walk the golden streets.
   Refrain

4. Then let our songs abound,
   And ev'ry tear be dry;
   We're marching thru Immanuel's ground,
   We're marching thru Immanuel's ground,
   To fairer worlds on high,
   To fairer worlds on high.
   Refrain

When the Roll Is Called Up Yonder

Registration 5
Rhythm: Shuffle or Swing

Words and Music by
James M. Black

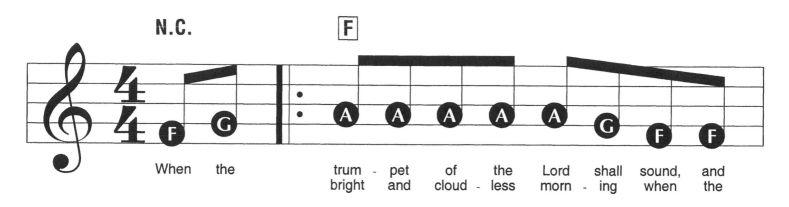

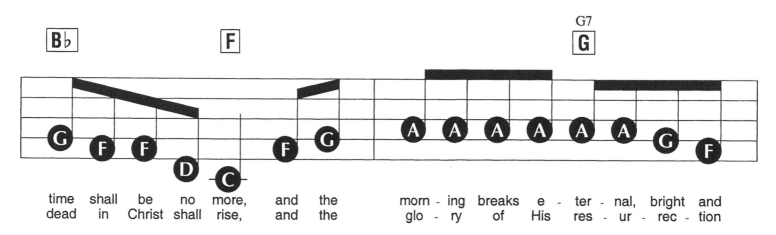

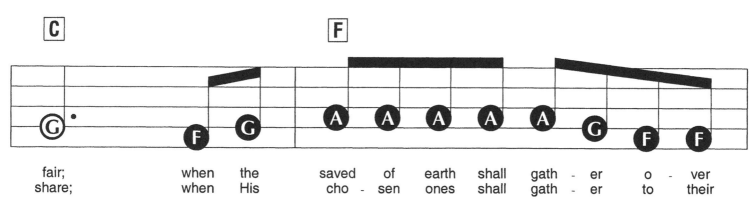

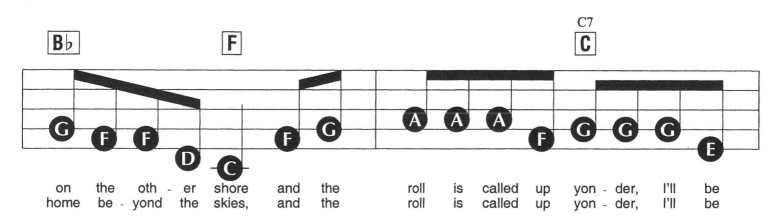

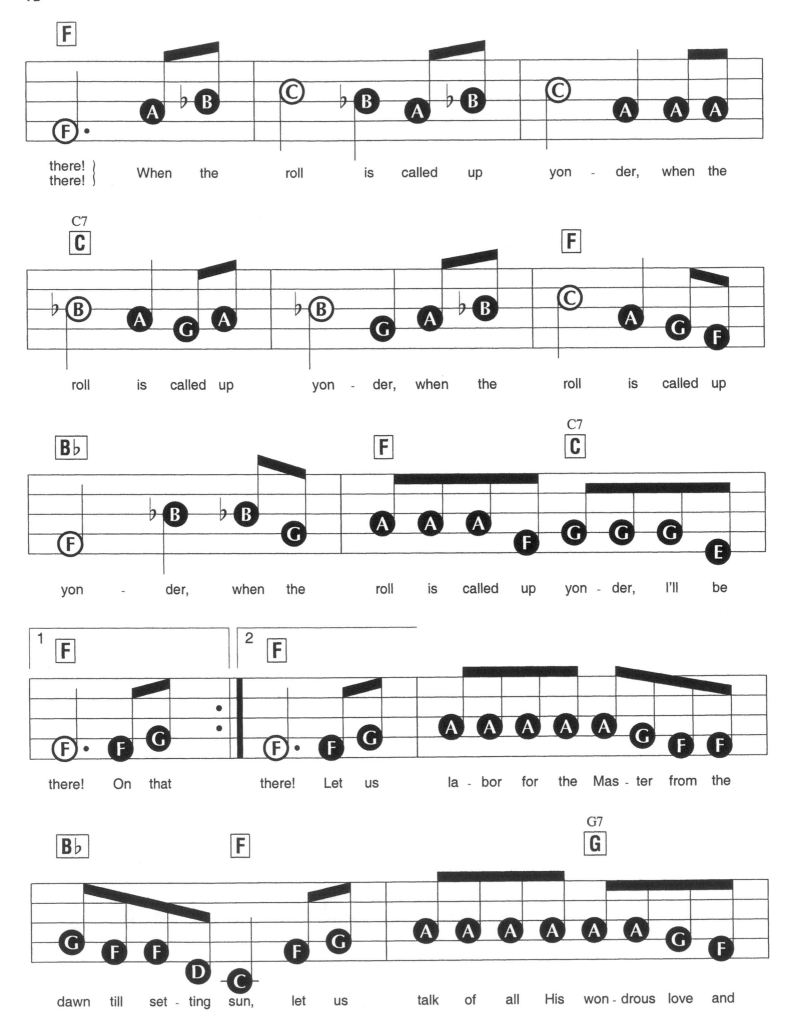

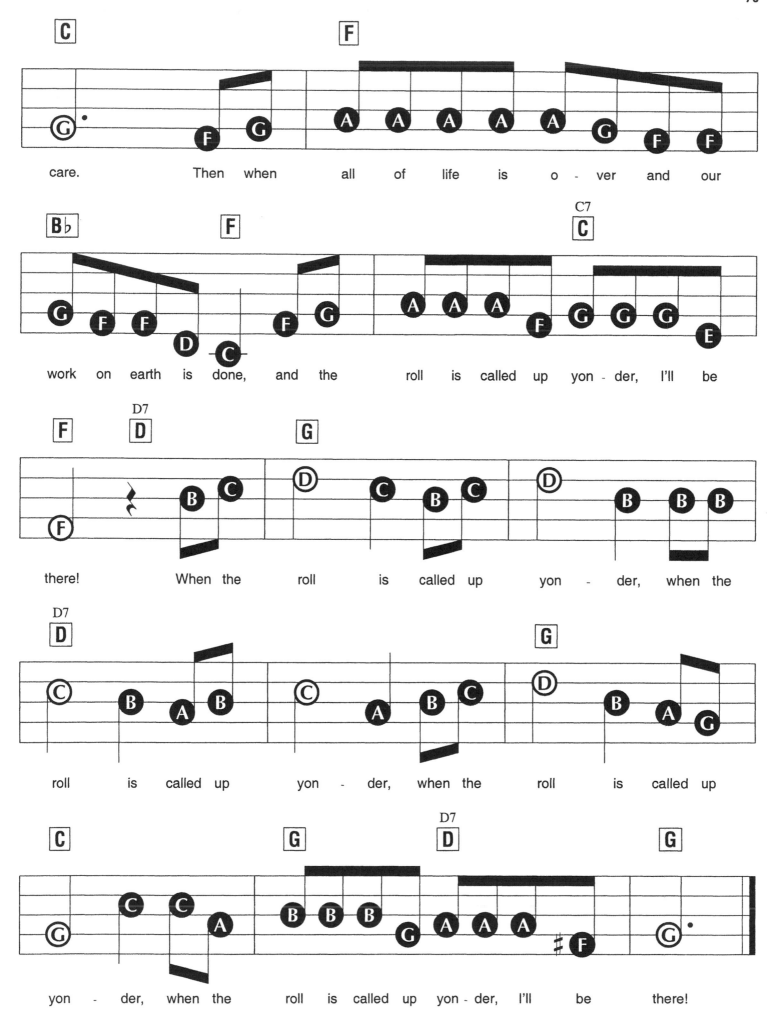

What a Friend We Have in Jesus

Registration 3
Rhythm: 8 Beat or Pops

Words by Joseph Scriven
Music by Charles C. Converse

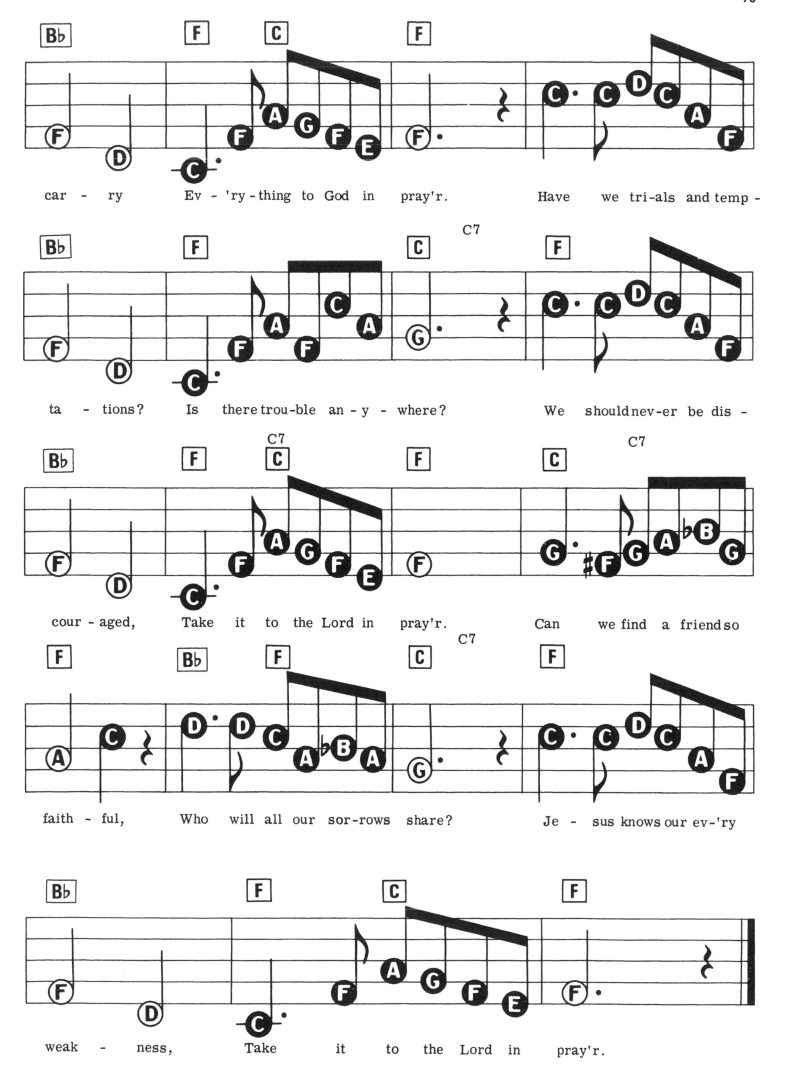

When We All Get to Heaven

Registration 4
Rhythm: Ballad or Fox Trot

Words and Music by E.E. Hewitt
and J.G. Wilson

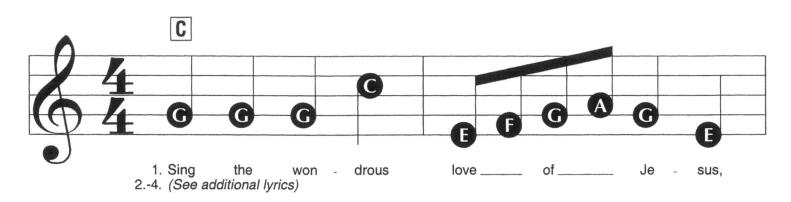

1. Sing the won-drous love _____ of _____ Je - sus,
2.-4. *(See additional lyrics)*

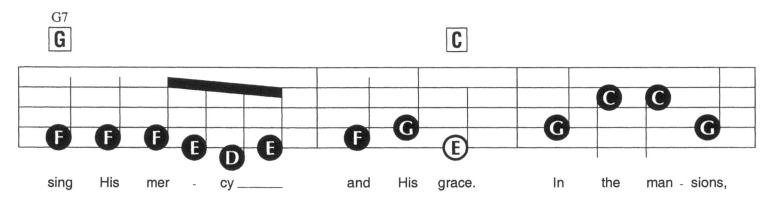

sing His mer - cy _____ and His grace. In the man - sions,

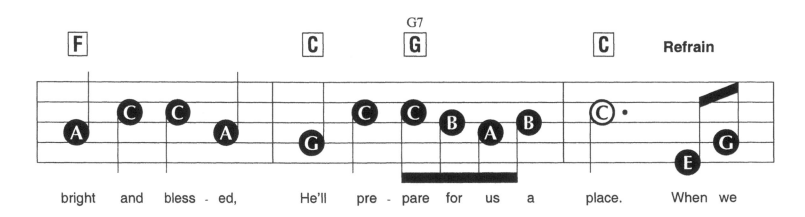

bright and bless - ed, He'll pre - pare for us a place. When we

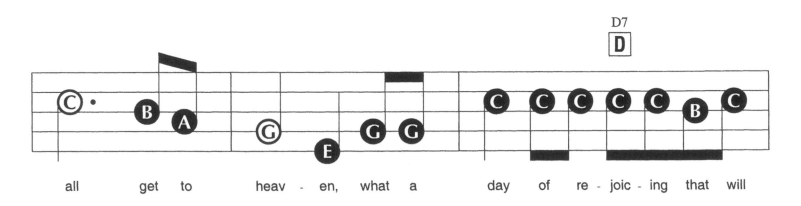

all get to heav - en, what a day of re - joic - ing that will

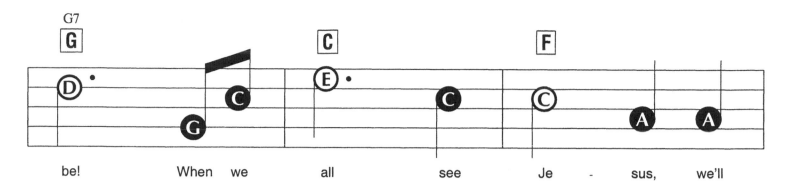

be! When we all see Je - sus, we'll

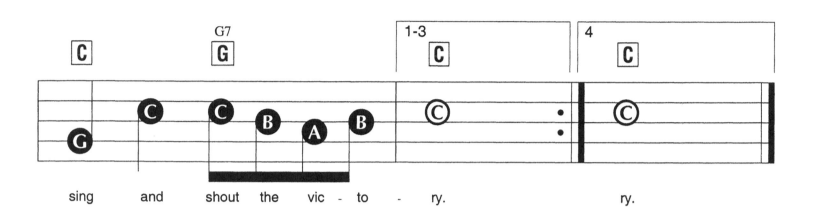

sing and shout the vic - to - ry. ry.

Additional Lyrics

2. While we walk the pilgrim pathway,
   Clouds will overspread the sky;
   But when trav'ling days are over,
   Not a shadow, not a sigh!
   Refrain

3. Let us then be true and faithful,
   Trusting, serving ev'ryday.
   Just one glimpse of Him in glory
   Will the toils of life repay.
   Refrain

4. Onward to the prize before us!
   Soon His beauty we'll behold.
   Soon the pearly gates will open;
   We shall tread the streets of gold.
   Refrain

Whiter Than Snow

Registration 10
Rhythm: Waltz

Words by James Nicholson
Music by William G. Fischer

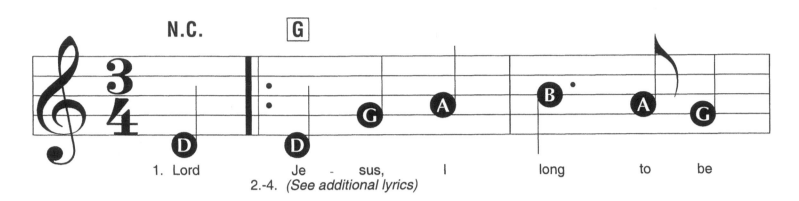

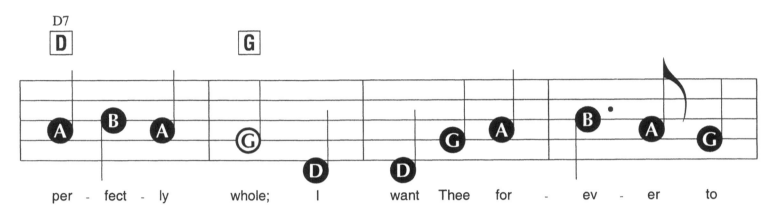

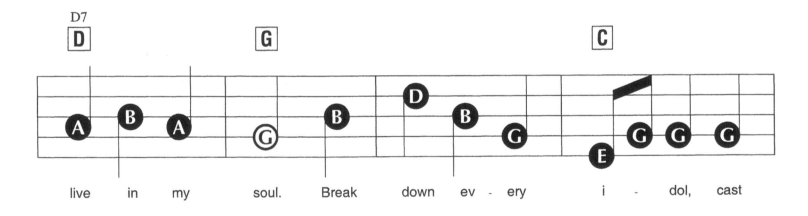

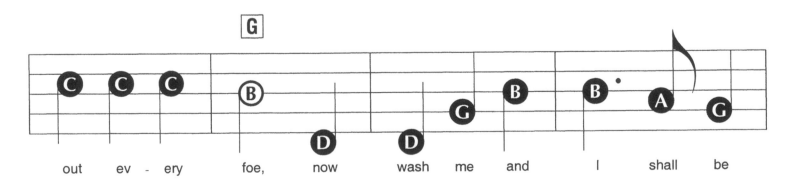

79

Refrain

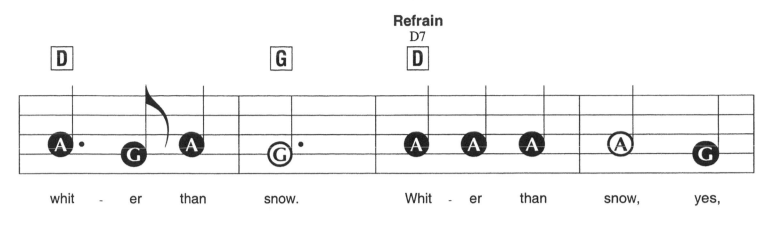

whit - er than snow. Whit - er than snow, yes,

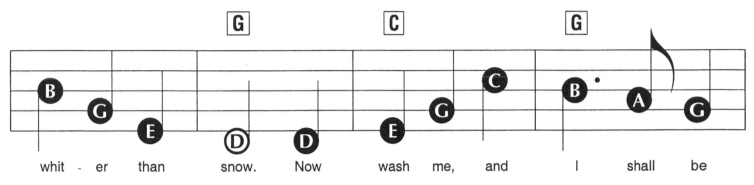

whit - er than snow. Now wash me, and I shall be

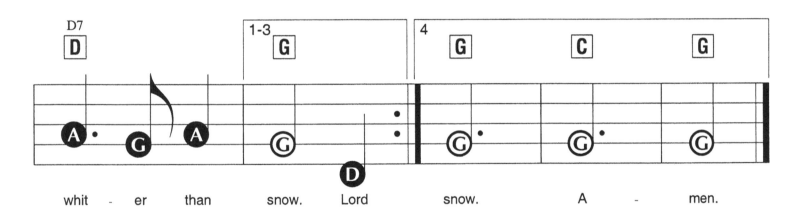

whit - er than snow. Lord snow. A - men.

Additional Lyrics

2. Lord Jesus, look down from Thy throne in the skies,
And help me to make a complete sacrifice;
I give up myself, and whatever I know,
Now wash me and I shall be whiter than snow.
Refrain

3. Lord Jesus, for this I most humbly entreat,
I wait, blessed Lord, at Thy crucified feet;
By faith, for my cleansing I see Thy blood flow,
Now wash me and I shall be whiter than snow.
Refrain

4. Lord Jesus, Thou seeest I patiently wait,
Come now, and within me a new heart create;
To those who have sought Thee, Thou never saidst "No,"
Now wash me and I shall be whiter than snow.
Refrain

Registration Guide

- Match the Registration number on the song to the corresponding numbered category below. Select and activate an instrumental sound available on your instrument.

- Choose an automatic rhythm appropriate to the mood and style of the song. (Consult your Owner's Guide for proper operation of automatic rhythm features.)

- Adjust the tempo and volume controls to comfortable settings.

Registration

1	Flute, Pan Flute, Jazz Flute
2	Clarinet, Organ
3	Violin, Strings
4	Brass, Trumpet
5	Synth Ensemble, Accordion, Brass
6	Pipe Organ, Harpsichord
7	Jazz Organ, Vibraphone, Vibes, Electric Piano, Jazz Guitar
8	Piano, Electric Piano
9	Trumpet, Trombone, Clarinet, Saxophone, Oboe
10	Violin, Cello, Strings